CW01475976

For my mum,

who showed me the magic in life.

Unconditional

Unforgettable

Unbreakable

KATEBRAZIER

A WEEK AT MEREDITH'S

by Kate Brazier

1

The mud stirs.

Woolly voices. Ringing.

Can't get there.

I sink.

It stirs again.

Kick up, up, up. Kick through the murk. Kick to the surface: warmth, light.

Pain.

On my back. Pressure on chest. Eyes stuck shut.

Rattling, humming, whooshing. Footsteps. Phone.

Exhaustion.

Can't move, can't open eyes. Blocked throat – can't speak.

Wheezy breathing. Warm hand, cold wetness. Sharp pinch. Injection? Pressure on wrist, murmuring.

Bright light. Tight arm.

Sinking again.

Please stop that phone ringing.

Pain wracks my muscles, my bones. Aching, throbbing, sore. Throat feels stuffed with straw. I picture a cartoon me, whacked back and forth over a cartoon strongman's head.

Phone answered: *'Bonjour.'*

French?

Like twisting a radio dial, memories flash in my mind: blue lights, screaming, pumping bass. Wet cobbles, fear.

Come on, Tana. Remember.

Awake again. My mind is much clearer. I hear birdsong. I am warm, in bed, but riddled with pain. My eyes are stuck. I can't move. There is something in my throat. Breathing feels strange. Ribs howl with every lungful. Am I in hospital?

Jack and Oliver. Where are they?

Sounds nearby: low-level electric humming. A hushed whirring. Comforting, calming, white noise; it whispers that machines are working. For me?

Sounds further away: a child's voice. A man's voice. The phone. The fast, flat slap of sandals. Coins rattling. A can clunking. The child cheering, the man laughing. Everyday sounds which don't include me. I am alone inside my body, inside my mind.

Clickety Click. Whoosh. What is that?

Light, squelchy footsteps approach my bed – it is a woman. She's wearing soft shoes. She sings quietly to herself and does not know I can hear her. Does not know I'm awake. She sings the same refrain over and over while pressing machine buttons – plasticky snicks and beeps. Something prints; she tears the paper and squelches from the room.

I sink under.

Metallic clattering wakes me. My mind is sharper; the mud is rinsing. Conversation drifts in but I only catch a few words: *'Café au lait'; 'thé'; 'croissant'; 'petit-déjeuner.'*

Why French? And why can't I move? And where are Jack and Oliver?

This time, thinking about my sons makes my palms and soles prickle. Anxiety's cold, familiar hand grabs my guts, and twists. Images flicker through my head: a ten-car pile-up, a terrorist attack, a brutal mugging. A train wreck or a plane crash. Anything could have happened.

I should breathe deep and slow, to stop panic slamming my chest and obliterating logical thought, but I feel sick, and my breathing is not my own. Perspective is sliding. Everything is wrong. Everyone I love is dead. I know this. Horror happened. Only I survived. My body is broken, and these French people think my mind is too.

I need to grab their attention. I must move, get up, run away, but when I try to shout that I am awake and scared and need help, an alarm starts wailing. Running footsteps, strangers surrounding me. A sharp scratch on my arm. Darkness rushes in.

Sunlight caresses my face. I'm cosy, in a pink world. Floaty. A human lava lamp, fluid and bright. No pain, just bliss. Wrapped and coddled, I bump off the walls and ceiling in my safe, fluffy bubble. Down to the floor, then up again. Slow motion. Calm.

Why was I scared? Can't remember. Stay peaceful, Tana, don't get ruffled. Not again. No way. No way, José. No way, not today. No panic. Just chill.

Clickety click. Whoosh.

That sound again. It chills my heart, prods my brain, reminds me. Of what? My parents' open fire? I liked poking embers. Toasting marshmallows. Using bellows, puffing flame from glowing coals.

No. Wrong memory. Push away the bad one.

Sleep.

The phone again. Pain ricochets around my body like a pinball. The room is darker. My mannequin's limbs need to move, but I still can't move them or open my eyes.

Keep trying, Tana, try harder.

Finally, my fingers wiggle – just a bit. My right hand rotates a little, the left hurts too much. My toes twitch. It's like moving through wet concrete, but these millimetre motions say I will heal.

The woman with squelchy footsteps comes back and fiddles with the machines. This time she is humming a classical tune. Probably from a TV advert because it makes me think of ice cream.

I tap the bed. Nothing.

I try to speak. Nothing.

Suddenly, a guttural grunt bursts from my throat. The humming stops. I repeat the sound. She gasps, and in three squelches reaches my bed. She lifts my wooden hand and squeezes.

'Tana?'

By way of reply, I wiggle my fingers weakly and she exclaims, starts speaking in rapid French. She feels my forehead, strokes my cheek, pats my hand. Still talking away, asking a million questions I don't understand and have no way of answering, she clicks another button. But she knows I'm awake.

Her language prompts memories: Meredith's house, the beach, Stefan, a neon nightclub. I'm still in France so Jack and Oliver must still be in England – safe – and that is all that matters. I wonder if they know I'm in hospital. Does Jamie know?

Clickety click, whoosh.

That sound again. Hearing it louder prods the memory I pushed away earlier. But I can't think about that. I won't think about it. Instead, I concentrate on the nurse's voice and her gentle hands. The lump in my throat stops me from talking, but I can make quiet grunting noises to show I am listening. My arms and legs are still dead, and my hands can only flop like two beached fish, yet she rambles on as if everything is great, talking as if we are having an actual conversation. She is kind. Reassuring.

Soon, more footsteps approach. Someone has those little metal things on their heels to stop them wearing down. *Tap tap tap.* They stop, presumably at my door, and a man speaks.

'*Oui,*' the nurse replies.

'*Bon.*'

He gives what I assume are orders in staccato bursts, and the others scatter. Even though I don't understand much French, it's obvious this man has authority. Maybe he is my consultant. But, despite sounding capable and confident, it's unsettling to be at his mercy.

'*Cinq minutes,*' he says, and his metallic tapping fades away.

The last thing I remember is being with Meredith, so is she in hospital too? Was it her I remember screaming? I have so many questions but no language and no voice. The fact that they know I'm awake isn't changing my isolation. Blood booms in my ears. I'm like a baby in the womb, except I am aware. It's claustrophobic. The booming gets louder, faster. I've had panic attacks before and know that adrenaline is soaking my bloodstream. My body wants to run or fight, but it's frozen.

Clickety click. Whoosh.

Push it away, push it away. The alarm starts wailing again – high-pitched, and fast. Last time, they drugged me up, but this time the nurse switches off the alarm. She strokes my hair and speaks in low, soothing tones, rubbing my arm, squeezing my hand.

'Shh, Tana. Ok, ok,' she whispers.

The alarm must be on a heart monitor, or something like that. I get her point. If I don't calm down, they will put me out again. But that is easier said than done – the *clickety click* memory is now clear: I am five and my grandad has cancer. He is lying in a hospital bed, smiling at me. I am scared. There is a hole in his throat. It's never been there before. A tube is helping him breathe. There's a flat disc covering the hole, and when he tries to talk it flaps open and closed. *Clickety click.* A machine pushes air into him. *Whoosh.* Grandad is tired and cross. He can only make words as he breathes out. He sounds funny, hard to understand. He is a robot.

Please don't tell me I have one of those metal tubes put in. I can't bear the thought of it. Yet the lump I can't cough up and the *whoosh* of the breathing machine says it's true. I've had a tracheotomy, just like grandad. A machine is breathing for me.

Clickety click. Whoosh.

Tears escape my stuck eyelids and run

sideways down my face. The nurse, with her gentle voice and soothing sounds, tries to make me feel better by stroking my hair and wiping my face, and I appreciate her efforts, I really do, but she can't do much. This is as bad as I can imagine.

2

As promised, about five minutes later the consultant's brisk footsteps tap through the corridor towards my room. I imagine him being in his early 50's, tall and thin, with dark curly hair and a neatly clipped moustache, wearing a suit and crisp white shirt, no tie. Polished brogues.

'Bonjour,' he says.

The nurse replies, no doubt explaining that I got upset and tripped the alarm on the machine.

'Oui,' he says. *'D'accord.'*

In four taps he is at the foot of my bed. I hear him wrestling the clipboard from its cage at the foot of my bed before asking the nurse a series of questions. The cadence of his voice goes up at the end of each sentence. She responds in more measured tones, purely professional. The pages rustle as he flips through my notes, questioning her all the time. I won't take my sight for granted anymore and neither will I underestimate listening.

Even though I can't understand what they're saying, I get the sense that she likes him.

It reminds me of something I read in an article about call centres, that staff are told to smile when answering the phone because it makes them sound friendlier. It must be true, because this nurse sounds like she's smiling. I can almost feel her blushing. Maybe he is handsome. Maybe she has a crush.

'*Bon,*' he says again. '*D'accord.*' Eventually he puts the clipboard back and addresses me. 'Tana,' he says, '*Je m'appelle –*'

I don't catch his name or what he says afterwards – his speech is way too fast for my ignorant ear, but it's not as if we can have a conversation, is it? I'm lying flat out, with my eyes stuck shut and a metal tube in my throat. However, we do find a way to communicate. It is pure, if painful: when he pinches my feet and toes, I manage a feeble toe wriggle. When he squeezes my muscles, I gurgle. His hands move slowly, traversing my body, and when he moves on to my hands and I feel his fingers, with short nails and a light dusting of hair, I can't help imagining them handling me in better circumstances.

But what am I thinking? This is no time for fantasy. Mr Whatever-his-name-is might be my saviour but, right now, he is trying to establish what damage I've done – what hurts and what works. If I could, I'd tell him in no uncertain terms that everything hurts, and nothing works.

As he runs his hands over me, assessing,

he dictates his findings to the nurse. Her pen scratches, and rolls. When he has finished, she peels the tape off my eyes and gently washes my face with a warm, damp cloth. Blinking helps the world slide into focus, and I understand the miracle of vision. Such a beautiful thing, taken for granted.

The doctor is younger and chunkier than I pictured, but quite tall, with cropped black hair, dark brown skin, and brown eyes. No moustache, just a little goatee. He wears a well-cut suit and his eyes crinkle in the corners when he smiles. He rambles on, forgetting that I don't understand.

At last, he says, *'Ah, pardon,'* and turns to the nurse. *'Elle ne comprend pas.'*

Ironically, this one I do.

Scratching his head, he blows out a deep breath, clearly exasperated by being unable to explain to me why I have a mutilated throat, useless limbs, and the weight of a small truck on my chest. He and the nurse have a brief conversation and I wish I had paid more attention in my French lessons at school, instead of staring out of the classroom window, watching the boys in my year play football.

Eventually he shrugs and pulls a little torch from his breast pocket. Raising one eyelid at a time, he blinds me for a moment, then holds his finger up and moves it from side to side, wanting me to follow. Next comes the stethoscope, which makes me moan like a bear when pressed on my chest.

'*Désolé.*'

He takes my pulse and my temperature, checks my forehead, my ribs – even examines my ears. Old school doctoring which is charming and reassuring. Peering at the contraption in my throat, he lifts the air away and my stomach flips, but he soon replaces it and adjusts the clip. Then he updates the nurse, and she writes everything down.

Finally, she hands him a clean needle which he jabs into my arm. It hurts and I groan, but he smiles and proceeds to jab me over and over, up and down both arms and legs. Finally, he lifts my left arm up, then lets it go. Obviously, it slaps back down. Disappointment flashes across his face. He studies me with his lips pressed together and a deep frown.

I don't know what to think – will I be like this forever?

Just as I begin imagining the rest of my life stuck in bed, he smiles, shrugs, and gives me a thumbs up. Then he speaks to the nurse, and she nods. She squeezes my hand again, and they leave the room without so much as a backwards glance. The door clicks shut behind them.

Great. I am none the wiser about why I am here, and they have deserted me. I can't move, I can't talk, I can't see into the corridor and, whilst the curtains in here are bright with sunshine, they are closed so I can't see outside either. I could be anywhere.

As far as hospital rooms go this one is as bland as you would expect. The cream walls could do with a fresh lick of paint. Two faded prints hang opposite my bed; one is five poppies in a yellow vase, the other is of a single pink peony. It is hanging crookedly. My bed is a standard hospital type with a solid metal foot, a controller for adjustments, and guard rails along both sides. They are down now, mocking my inability to escape.

The door is to my left and the clock above reads eleven fifteen, but I don't know what the date is – I have no idea how long I've been in here. The window is on my right. Beneath it is a wheeled table, with a small pile of magazines and a vase of orange carnations on top. A scuffed armchair lurks in the corner. In my peripheral vision I can see a beige cabinet to the left of the bed; it holds a box of tissues, a water jug, a plastic beaker, and a bowl of red grapes. Dangling from a tall metal stand on my right is a bag of clear liquid, with an IV line running from it into my wrist. It must be that hydration fluid they use when you can't eat or drink, which means I must have a catheter too, and a bag of urine hanging somewhere.

Classy.

Did Meredith bring the grapes and flowers? Did she sit in the armchair, reading magazines while I slept? Maybe her friends came too. Being watched while unconscious is a dreadful thought – worse than having no visitors at all.

The ensuite bathroom door gapes wide, and a lightbox which must be on the wall behind me is reflected in the mirror above the sink. Two X-ray images are on display: my ribcage and my skull. Who else would they belong to? Now I'm no expert, but the skull has no obvious signs of injury. That's great, but three of the ribs are cracked. No wonder my chest hurts so much.

When I am strong enough to get out of this bed and into the bathroom, what other horrors will that mirror reveal? The tracheotomy tube will have to come out and I'll probably have a scar there forever, but maybe I have other injuries too. Some might be internal. Some might be permanent. I may have more scars.

The X-rays steal the joy I felt at getting my sight back. What have I got to be glad about? I can't move, I'm all alone, and I have no idea what the hell happened. Where is Meredith? And does anyone know I'm here? Does anyone even care?

Angry tears well. It's obvious that I can't go home until I regain full movement, so I am determined to speed that process up. My body feels like it is thawing from the extremities inwards – I can make small movements with my hands, but it is exhausting and infuriating, and even my head is being stubborn and ignoring my orders to turn. I have a lot of work to do. Nobody else can do this for me.

I go on and on, trying and trying, willing my head to move and then, finally, perseverance pays dividends. Around midday my head moves, just a smidge in each direction. Doing so pulls on my ruined throat, but I keep on, practising and practising. All progress is good progress.

By twelve thirty I am shattered, with not even the energy to cry. I am spun and wrung and hung out to dry. My world has changed, maybe forever. When did this all start? At what point in my almost-thirty years did I step onto the travelator which has dumped me here, in France, broken and alone, hundreds of miles from everyone I love?

3

This diary is the private property of Tana Davis.
KEEP YOUR NOSE OUT!

Sunday, April 20th, 1997
Dear Diary,
Scott had a party last night because his parents went away for the weekend – to celebrate their anniversary or something. His house got trashed. Drinks were spilt, the sofa got burnt, people were in the beds, and someone smeared cat food on the kitchen ceiling.

We found it hilarious, but Scott's brother went mad. He's old, he's like 23, so thought he could tell us what to do. He kept kicking people out but was too stupid to realise that they just went round the side and came back in through the kitchen door. Nobody admitted to doing the ceiling, but it smelt gross, and the cat spent all night sitting on the counter, staring up, licking his lips. Sarah was laughing so hard I thought she might wet herself. It wouldn't be the first time.

Scott's parents have a great sound system, and the music was so loud I kept expecting the police to turn up like they did last summer when Melissa had a party, but they didn't, thankfully. The best bit was when someone put "Smells Like Teen Spirit" on, and we were all jumping about and yelling, playing air drums to see who could do the best impression of Dave Grohl. It was so much fun. The strobe light made it look like we were doing it in slow motion, which was so cool!

I'd love to have a party here, but Mum and Dad would kill me. Like, actual death. I know this. It's because in Newquay there is no chance of any party being small. Scott only invited a few of us originally but word got around like it always does and, in the end, there must've been about a hundred people in his house. As usual though, no boys worth snogging.

Also as usual, Sarah was hammered. She stole two cans of beer from her dad's fridge and downed them, then raided Scott's parents' drinks cabinet for gin, vodka, and anything else that was open. She told me she was 'on a mission to get shitfaced.' She'll blame me for her hangover, I know she will, but she's not my responsibility and I can't stop her from doing this every time we go out. Her behaviour is predictable and boring. One minute she was getting off with Daniel, who she's been stalking for weeks, then five minutes later she was being sick. I took her outside to get some fresh air and she puked all over the daffodils.

She said, 'Tana, will Daniel still like me?

Why did you let me get so drunk? I feel really …
bleugghhh!'

Let her? Seriously, I couldn't have stopped
her without a straitjacket. She was on her hands
and knees in the flowerbed, and I was holding
her hair back, but I held it right at the ends so
she wouldn't puke on my shoes. She was kind
of swinging about. At one point she swung off
sideways and banged her face on the bird bath.
I had to laugh – it serves her right. If she has a
bruise, I'll deny all knowledge.

Sarah can be an idiot sometimes. She
deliberately mixed a load of different spirits, and
that's just stupid. Still, at least she didn't take any
drugs. Not as far as I know, anyway. Tom was
selling those Smiley Face acid tabs and loads of
people took one, but Tom must have taken a few
because he was out of his tree. Just before we left,
I saw him sitting cross-legged under the table in
the utility room, talking to a cat poo in the litter
tray. I mean, what the hell? I can't understand the
attraction of getting off your head. Not if that's
the result.

Newquay might be my home but it's too
intense for me. I'm leaving as soon as I can – it's
all planned in my head. Next month, my GCSEs
start. Then it's the summer. Some of my friends
want to get jobs straight away but I am going to
sixth form in September to do A levels, and then
I'm going to university. I'll choose somewhere
miles away, far from Mum and Dad's tight leash.

Who knows where I'll end up? Maybe Scotland. Maybe Spain. Maybe Australia. I'm going to be a lawyer.

Sarah laughs at me when I say that, but all she cares about is boys, and the boys at school are boring. Fun enough to watch when I'm stuck in lessons and they've got PE, but they're all way too immature to be boyfriend material. Besides, most of them are like Sean, who I liked until he called me fat and frigid because I wouldn't have sex with him. He talked Lucy into it and then bragged to his friends, told them all the details. For weeks they called her a slag and treated Sean like some kind of hero. Yuk. I definitely don't need boys like that in my life.

I'll write again soon.

This diary is the private property of Tana Davis. KEEP YOUR NOSE OUT!

Wednesday, May 21st, 1997
Dear Diary,
For the last five weeks I've been almost dying of pneumonia, which is why I haven't written – but something even more gigantic than that happened! I can hardly believe it.

It all started the day after Scott's party, which was, at first, a normal, boring, freezing Sunday. In the afternoon, I was snuggled under a blanket on the sofa, reading, when Mum came in and ordered me to take Barney out. I refused, obviously.

She gave me the Raised Eyebrow of Doom and said, 'Tana, he's your dog. You wanted him, you walk him.'

'Don't be mean, Janice,' I said, to wind her up. 'It's horrible outside.'

'Less of that Janice nonsense, young lady.' Her eyebrow was literally climbing up her head.

I wrapped my blanket tighter and pulled a stressed face, made my voice all whiny. 'But it's too cold! It's really windy.'

'Rubbish.' She put her hands on her hips, so I knew she meant business. 'German Shepherds love this weather, and the sea air is bracing. It's good for you.'

Bracing. Where does she get these words? Anyway, arguing was futile so I took him, and we ended up at Fistral Beach. The waves were roaring. Barney found a massive stick and barked until I threw it, and every time he dropped it at my feet, his happy, furry face made me laugh. But then I noticed a surfer, right up at the north end near the rocks. He was very talented – even I could see it and I know nothing about surfing. There was something mesmerising about the way he moved, so I kept watching him while throwing Barney's stick.

It was pouring with rain by this time and the wind was so strong it was almost blowing me off my feet, but I kept watching the surfer and throwing the stick for Barney. Suddenly though, the surfer fell. I looked for him, but the waves were constant. He was nowhere. I felt sick, thinking he had whacked his head on his surfboard and was drowning, but nobody else was around and the nearest phone box is up on the main road, so I figured if I ran there and called the coastguard, he would be dead before they arrived.

I was a bit panicky. My hair was whipping around my face, Barney was barking, wanting me to throw the stick for him again, and I was almost crying with indecision. Then I figured there was nothing else for it – I would have to rescue him myself. I stripped off, down to my underwear, right there on the beach, and waded in.

Oh my God, I have never felt anything like it. As soon as the water swallowed my feet, I was covered in goosebumps and gasping for breath, but I kept going until it was up to my waist. I was having one of those internal conversations where 99.9% of my brain was screaming at me to get dressed and go home, and the rest said to shut up and get on with it because a man's life was at stake. The waves and spray were soaking me anyway, there was no point coming back out, so I scanned the water one last time. Even though I still couldn't see him, I took a deep breath and dived under.

It was like diving into needles. I remember thinking I could have a heart attack, but by that time I was fully in, so started swimming. The whole thing was crazy. It was freezing, there could have been a rip tide, nobody knew I was there, and the current was strong, but I kept swimming. If I had found him, I've no idea what I thought I would be able to do. I am no lifeguard and know zero about lifesaving, but still, I kept swimming.

Barney was barking and jumping about in the shallow water, wanting me to come back, but I swam out and out, looking for the guy. After a while though, my energy disappeared. It just vanished. I couldn't feel my limbs or breathe properly, and there was nothing to see; the surfer was nowhere. The colder I got, the more my imagination went wild, and I kept thinking he would pop up in front of me, like something out of *Jaws 3D*, all dead and frightening. So, I turned around and headed back to the shore.

I almost didn't make it. Even though I wasn't far out, it felt like miles. The rain, wind, waves, and killer cold was almost too much – I crawled out of the water and flopped onto the sand, where Barney bounced around, barking, and licking my face. He was trying to get me up, but exhaustion held me down. He must have realised because he shook himself off and lay down next to me. He's such a grizzly – I cuddled up to him for warmth and shut my eyes, trying to summon the strength to get dressed.

Then I heard, 'Hello? Are you alright?'

I thought I was having a near death experience. Opening my eyes, I saw long, wet-suited legs and the bottom of a surfboard. I wondered how the dead surfer could be standing in front of me, talking. Not only that but he looked freakishly tall because I was lying flat.

'What were you thinking,' he said, 'going for a swim when it's so cold? You should at least be wearing a wetsuit.'

Barney looked back and forth from me to the man, but he wasn't growling or responding in any other way, which made it even weirder. My head was whirling, and I wondered why he was annoyed with me, when I had tried to rescue him. What was his problem? I sat up and wrapped my arms around my knees. 'Are you a ghost?'

His whole face lit up as he laughed, and I realised he was super good looking. 'No, I'm real, but you're blue and need to get warm,' he said.

I told him that I went in to save him. That I thought he was drowning.

He frowned. 'Save me? I'm fine.'

'But you fell off. You didn't come up and nobody was here.' I shook my head, frustrated that he didn't understand, and waved loosely towards the road. 'Phone's miles away – I had to rescue you.'

'Are you a lifeguard?'

'No. I just thought … I thought –' My words dried on my wet lips. Then tears came and I sat, like a fool, shaking with cold and sobbing.

He coughed gently. When I looked up, he was smiling, but not in a nasty way. Just bemused.

'I did fall off,' he said, 'and my board banged me on the head. I went under for a few seconds and was a bit stunned, so clung on and let the current take me until I stopped seeing stars. I ended up much further down the beach.' I stared at him. 'That's why you couldn't see me. The waves are moving fast, they took me all the way down there.' He pointed far away to the other end of Fistral. 'It took less than a minute. It's a strong current today. Great surf.'

Barney sat beside me, a soggy, fluffy mountain of comfort. Slinging one arm across him and snuggling in close, I rested my forehead on my knees and closed my eyes, willing the shame away. The surfer man walked off without another word, but in a couple of minutes he was back, holding my clothes.

Pulling a towel from his bag, he said, 'You need to get warm.' The towel was soft and thick, and I caught a waft of freshness as he wrapped it around me. 'This will have to do. I wish I had one of those silver emergency blankets though – that's what you really need.'

The colour began to fade from everything. The man looked grey and indistinct. All I wanted was to sleep. I leaned into Barney, who licked my face.

'I need to get you home – in fact I think you need to go to hospital,' the man said, rubbing the water off my arms and legs with another towel. 'Sorry if this is a bit rough but I'm trying to get your blood moving. You're a very strange colour.'

Then he started dressing me. On one level, it felt dreamy, like watching a romantic comedy I was starring in. On another, I was mortified. He dried my feet and legs, pulled my jeans up to my knees and laced my boots.

'Lie back and lift your bum up, so I can get these on you.'

I couldn't feel my toes but pushed down onto the sand and arched my back. He squatted beside me, yanked my 501s up, and even buttoned them because my fingers were like raw chipolatas. There was nothing attractive about being soaked and freezing in old, ugly underwear, but the guy didn't seem to notice. He dressed me, then rubbed Barney's massive head, called him a beauty, and said he would drive us home. Barney licked his hand, and I knew I was safe.

Somehow, the surfer man packed up all his stuff, practically carried me across the beach to carpark, even though he was also carrying his surfboard, and put me in his car. Barney jumped into the back. I passed out right after telling him my address.

I can't remember getting home or how Mum and Dad reacted, but they took me to hospital, and I woke up the next morning feeling like death. The doctors said I had mild hypothermia. Then I got pneumonia and have never felt so ill. Still, all I could think about was the handsome surfer.

A few days later, a bouquet of flowers arrived. *To my brave rescuer*, the card read. *I hope you're feeling better – from Jamie*.

Mum said the flowers were from him. I can only imagine her face when she opened the door to a tall stranger dressed in a wetsuit, who had her only child slumped in the front seat of his car. She must have been horrified but, typical Janice, still managed to find out about him. Jamie lives in Bristol and had driven down to Cornwall for a weekend of surfing.

'He said that he comes down to Newquay often, Tana. He has family here. Naturally, I asked him who, but didn't recognise the surname – Malone. Do you know anyone with that name?'

I don't, but she's unbelievable, the way she gets information out of people. I bet she asked him loads of questions, even though she hasn't told me much. Nothing I want to know anyway, like how old he is and whether he's got a girlfriend.

Jamie Malone. I like the way his name sounds, the way it rolls off the tongue. Tana

Malone … argh what am I thinking? I don't even know the guy – I probably wouldn't recognise him if I walked past him in the street. Well, maybe I would, because he was blonde and lovely, but the fact remains that I know nothing about him, other than the fact that he surfs and lives miles away. He might come to Newquay often, but I bet I'll never see him again. My big knickers would have scared him off. They would scare anyone off. He probably thinks I'm just some stupid kid.

Will write soon!

4

This diary is the private property of Tana Davis.
KEEP YOUR NOSE OUT!

Saturday, May 24th, 1997
Dear Diary,
Jamie the surfer rang me yesterday; he looked up my number!

I shouldn't have told him I've had pneumonia because he said it was his fault. Why would he think that? If he hadn't helped me, I could have died on that beach, and I said so, but he kept saying sorry. Unbelievable. None of the boys I know apologise for anything. That shows how mature Jamie is. He is really nice too; we talked for about ten minutes. He's twenty. Almost four years older than me. A proper man, with a job and a flat which he shares with some guy called Bradley. My chest felt all fluttery when he gave me his number and said I could call him if I wanted. If I wanted?!

First thing this morning, I called. Bradley answered and said, 'And who might you be?' in some silly, posh voice when I asked to speak to

Jamie.

I said my name and he repeated it three times, totally dropped the voice. 'Tana? That's a weird name.' So, Jamie obviously hadn't told him about me. 'He is here, but he's otherwise engaged.'

Immediately, I imagined Jamie waving at Bradley to get rid of whoever was on the phone. I pictured him with a girl there, kissing her, completely engrossed. 'Well, please can you tell him I rang?' He has my number.' Even I heard the disappointment in my voice.

Half an hour later, the phone rang. 'Sorry about Bradley,' Jamie said. 'I was in the shower.'

With that mental image dancing in my head, I don't even know what we talked about.

Anyway, Sarah came round at lunchtime. She was going to sleep over, but we had an argument. When I told her about calling Jamie, she rolled her eyes and said, 'What did you do that for?'

'Because I like him.'

'You're making a fool of yourself. Why would he be interested in you?'

'Thanks.' I could barely look at her.

'Listen,' she said, 'Think about it logically. He's older, he's got his own place, and if he's as good looking and lovely as you say, he must have a girlfriend. He might have two. He could be one of those guys who has loads of girls on the go at the same time. You know, a real player. Besides, he lives miles away. Forget about him.'

Why is she like that? How can she give me relationship advice, when she chases after the childish boys in our year and thinks that having an occasional snog when drunk equals romance?

Jealous, I think.

I told her not to slam the door on her way out.

I'll write with another update soon.

This diary is the private property of Tana Davis.
KEEP YOUR NOSE OUT!

Friday, June 6th, 1997

Dear Diary,

Mum and Dad have been yelling about the phone bill, stuff like, 'It's going to be huge, Tana, so you'd better get yourself a job, pronto!'

I said they should be glad that I'm happy, but all I got was pursed lips and raised eyebrows. Parents are weird.

The phone bill might be huge but talking to Jamie is becoming my favourite thing to do. He is so interesting – his life is so different to mine. I asked about his job, and he sighed. He said he works in banking, but that it's mostly just sitting in front of a computer, making phone calls. Said there wasn't much to say about it.

I can't imagine going to work every day and not having all the school holidays. How would I cope with not having my summers free? That is why I want to do something interesting, not something I just settle for, which is the situation Jamie's in.

I'm not judging him, but it sounds awful, and not much like banking, either, if you ask me. I thought people who work in banks stand behind those counters and serve customers: *'cashier number three, please,'* and give people their money or cash cheques, but Jamie said telephone banking is really popular. Shows how much I know.

Anyway, he prefers to hear about my life, my friends, and the stupid things that happen at school because my stories trigger memories about his school days, which he says he misses. I did an impression of Lucy impersonating Miss Wilson – the one she got a detention for – and he belly laughed. It was a nice feeling to know he thought I was funny too.

He tells me stories too though; the one about the time his "terrifying" Head of PE caught him and five friends smoking when they were bunking a lesson made me laugh so much I snorted. Too busy talking about football, they didn't realise that this teacher, Mr Carter, was watching them.

'Get lost on your way to Physics, did you,

boys?'

They all jumped and flicked their cigarettes away, except this one kid nicknamed Hairy Andy. In a panic, he dropped his cigarette down the inside of his shirt and set fire to his chest hair. Jamie was cracking up, remembering how Andy kept denying he'd been smoking, as grey smoke wafted out of his collar. All they could smell was burning. I tried to cover my snort with a cough, but Jamie just laughed harder. I'm glad he couldn't see how red I went.

I guess working doesn't have as much opportunity for fun as school does, but Jamie notices details about people which amuse him. Like, at his work there's a guy called Ajay who says, 'No!' and looks surprised whenever anyone tells him anything, and a woman called Ruthie who constantly twirls a piece of her hair and tucks it behind her ear. His boss's bald head is apparently covered in flecks of dry skin (gross!) He also told me about his flatmate Bradley's annoying, clingy girlfriend, and how she makes loads of noise when they have sex. He did an impression of her, and I laughed, but mostly out of embarrassment. When he said he bought earplugs to block her noise out, I didn't know what to say.

These observations mean he noticed my old, grey underwear on the beach. And my cellulite. There's no way that he could have missed either of those things. Still, I don't know why that bothers me; we are just friends, nothing more. I am probably too young for him – he wouldn't be interested. Would he?

I can hope.

I can wish.

Soon my GCSEs will be finished, and I'll have the entire summer to myself. Maybe Jamie will come back down to Newquay … I spend too much time hoping and wishing for that.

This diary is the private property of Tana Davis.
KEEP YOUR NOSE OUT!

Tuesday, June 17th, 1997

Dear Diary,

It's all kicked off. Dad isn't happy about me and Jamie talking so much.

He said, 'Jamie is an adult, Tana. A young man. He should stick to women his own age.'

My belly felt all hot and I wanted to tell him to fuck off, to stick his opinions, but I didn't – he would have killed me for swearing. But what annoys me most is that he and Mum are acting like I'm doing something terrible, and I'm not. I'm just talking to my friend.

They have never had any reason to be angry with me before, not really, and it's not as if I am deliberately winding them up. So why should

I stop talking to Jamie, just because they're worried and think it's 'inappropriate'? The other night, they told me to sit down because they wanted to have 'a little chat.' I plonked myself into the armchair and stared out the window.

Mum started. She said, 'Jamie seems like a nice lad.' She admitted it was lovely of him to bring me home that day, then added that it should have stopped there. I felt my fists clench when I turned to look at her and she was fake smiling. 'Brian?' she said. 'Anything to add?'

Dad nodded without even looking at me and said, 'He's twenty.'

Mum's smile dropped. In classic Janice style, she raised her eyebrows and peered at me over the top of her glasses. Like I don't know how old he is, or what they're implying. But I'll be seventeen in a few months; it's not that much of a difference. Is it?

When I didn't respond, Mum launched two classic lines: 'You'll get hurt,' and, 'he could be married with a child.'

Duh, yeah, of course he is. That is why he's on the phone to me nearly every night – he rings me while his wife's putting the baby to bed.

Unbelievable.

Mum can be an idiot. I told her she is paranoid and has been reading too many of those cheap magazines she loves so much.

She tutted, like she does, and said, 'It's lucky that you know best. Having all the answers must be wonderful.'

I gave her a death stare and went to my room, but later, when I snuck into the kitchen to make a mug of tea, she sniffed me out and started again.

'You're very young, darling. You have no experience. The age difference is huge, at this time in your life. Young men like Jamie, well, they want … *certain things*.' I almost spat my tea out.

Dad appeared in the doorway and chimed in too. 'Be sensible, darling,' he said. 'If it's necessary for you to have a boyfriend, why don't you ask Roger to go to the pictures with you? He's a nice boy – and he's your age.'

Then I did spit my tea out. Roger is perfectly nice, it's true. He is a sweet boy. Which is the reason I would never, ever, *ever* even contemplate considering him as boyfriend material. Not to mention the fact that I have known him since we were in nappies, or that he is a geeky twit whose popularity at school registers below zero – and that's with the people who know he exists. Just because he's their friends' son they think it's a great idea to pair us up.

It will never happen. Ever. Seriously, what red blooded sixteen-year-old would choose a weedy little nerd over a gorgeous hunk of a man? It's a no-brainer. My parents live in another universe.

I didn't want to make them angrier though,

so nodded and made a murmuring sound. They can take it for agreement if they want to interpret it that way. But I also told them that they can't stop me from talking to Jamie.

'We can, if we think you're in danger,' Mum said. Dad nodded and produced Serious Frown Face.

'In danger from what, exactly?' I asked. 'My ear dropping off because it's had a phone pressed against it for too long? Or maybe his imaginary wife coming to Cornwall and beating me up?'

'Don't be facetious, Tana,' Mum said. She sniffed and pursed her lips, looking to Dad for support. 'Brian? Do you have anything to say on the matter?'

'Don't speak to your mother like that,' he said, then scurried away to rearrange the shoe cupboard, or whatever the fuck he does to avoid conflict.

They can't stop me. I will do what I want – I don't care what they think. Even though he's older than me and lives miles away, Jamie and I can still speak. There is no harm in it.

Will update you soon!

This diary is the private property of Tana Davis.
KEEP YOUR NOSE OUT!

Wednesday, July 9th, 1997

Dear Diary,

Thank you, universe, thank you moon, and thank you stars. Thank you, to all the deities … Jamie is back in Cornwall.

Last night we were talking, and he dropped into the conversation that he would be driving down first thing this morning. He's staying all weekend. My whole body went hot, then cold, and a million questions fired all at once in my head: What will I wear? Have I got any spots? Have I lost weight? Have I got any nice underwear?

Cartwheeling around my room seemed the only sensible way to burn all the sudden energy, but of course I had to act calm. 'Oh, that's great,' I said. 'Maybe we can meet up? If you want to, that is.'

'Definitely,' he said. 'You're half the reason I'm coming.'

Explosions went off in my stomach and I was glad he couldn't see me punching the air. 'Only half?'

'The other half is surfing, obviously.'

What we talked about after that, I haven't a clue. Just one thing was revolving around my head: he likes me he likes me he likes me.

I debated not telling Mum and Dad but, in the end, figured I should. They get on my nerves, but I don't like lying to them. Jamie is twenty, and I must keep reminding myself that he's too old to be interested in me as a girlfriend. We are just friends.

When I mentioned his visit to Mum, she surprised me. 'Invite him round. We'll have afternoon tea.'

Replaying her words over and over, I searched for sarcasm but couldn't hear any. Thoughts included: why would she suddenly want him to come here? What is she planning? Maybe they've realised there's no point trying to stop us from keeping in touch. Or maybe she and Dad want to suss him out properly. There were so many options buzzing around my brain, but I decided I didn't care. I was just glad she invited him.

My stomach was in knots all night. This morning, I got up early, but it still took ages to shower, wash my hair, put on a bit of makeup, and cover two massive zits which appeared overnight. Typical. I'm sure my skin conspires against me.

Last time we met I was semi-conscious in my bra and big knickers so I knew that, really, anything other than that scenario would be a bonus, but deciding what to wear was still like trying to do quadratic equations while juggling. I changed my outfit at least six times before opting for my old favourites of faded 501's, a white T shirt, my pink Converse high-tops, and a squirt of CK1 perfume. It wasn't even ten o'clock.

'Take Barney for a walk, Tana,' Dad said. 'You're going to wear out the carpet.'

When Jamie finally rang the doorbell, I thought I was going to faint. Or be sick. Or both. Although we've talked loads on the phone, I hadn't seen him since the day we met.

He looked even better than I remembered. He's around six feet tall, slim but muscular, with tanned arms and an open face. Kind. His thick, fair hair is a bit too long and scruffy where it curls around his neck. Couldn't look more like a surfer if he tried.

It's weird because I've never paid any attention to guys like him – Newquay is full of them in the summer – but I imagined grabbing a handful of his hair, tipping his head back and snogging his face off.

'Tana, aren't you going to say hello?' Mum was standing to one side, holding the door open so Jamie could come in. But he was waiting for me to say something, and I was just staring at him, imagining what his mouth tastes like.

'Hi. Come in, please.' My cheeks were burning, and I wondered if he could tell what I'd been thinking, whether Mum and Dad could too. I could hardly breathe when I saw he was wearing Levi's, a thin, oatmeal-coloured jumper, and Vans. It is so cute that we wear the same kind of clothes.

We sat in the front room with Mum and

Dad. The coffee table was loaded with Mum's favourite China tea set – the one with little flowers painted around the edges. She had whipped up a selection of tiny sandwiches and cakes and was ready to hold court. I should have known she'd do something like that to me.

With clammy armpits and trembly hands, I perched on the edge of my chair, on full alert, but Jamie relaxed back into his chair, legs straight out in front, crossed at the ankles. He looked like he'd been coming round here for years.

'Brian and I really wanted to thank you, Jamie, for bringing Tana home that day,' Mum said. She poured tea into his cup and held up the milk jug, eyebrows raised in question. Jamie nodded and she added milk, then handed him the cup and saucer. 'Although why exactly she went into the sea, remains a matter of some confusion.'

'Mum!' I said, 'I've explained a thousand times that I thought he was drowning.'

She gave me a hard look through narrowed eyes. 'Yes, apparently so.'

Jamie laughed – at ease with Mum in a way I can never be. 'Honestly, Janice, we literally met there and then. It was as much of a shock to me as it was to you.' He smiled and she returned it, touched her hair.

'So, Jamie,' Dad said. He smiled in that interrogative way he has. 'What do you do for a living? Tana said something about a bank – is that right?'

I cringed – it's such a dad thing to ask – but Jamie was fine. He said it's telephone banking and that he has worked there since finishing his A levels.

'Oh, you stayed on at school then?' I thought Dad was impressed, until he said, 'Didn't fancy university though, eh? Getting a degree wasn't for you?'

My heart sank but Jamie smiled. 'Well, I might have gone to university, if it had been an option. But it wasn't. I needed to move out, so had to get a job.'

'You moved out at eighteen?' Dad frowned and glanced at Mum.

'Nineteen. Yes, I left as soon as I could.'

'That must have been challenging for you – leaving your family.'

Jamie shrugged. 'Not particularly. The thing is, Brian, not everyone is as lucky as Tana when it comes to parents.'

Privately, I disagreed – Jamie has no idea how annoying they are – but Dad beamed.

All I wanted was for my parents to leave the room so we could talk alone, but after an hour Mum was still fussing. She refilled the teapot and replenished the miniature cakes and sandwiches.

'Have another, Jamie,' she said, offering them. 'If you're surfing later, you'll need the energy, and I made these especially for you.'

'How can I refuse?' he said, piling up his plate. 'They're amazing; you should open a shop.'

Mum said, 'Oh!' and patted her hair again.

I couldn't eat anything and didn't say much either. My tongue was knotted. Mum and Dad, however, seemed to be enjoying his company too much to leave us in peace. They fired questions in tag-team fashion, probably hoping to find a weak spot, but Jamie managed them well. I struggled to concentrate on the details of their conversation though for several reasons:

1. Dad asked work-related questions I didn't understand and all I could think about was seeing Jamie naked.
2. Mum asked about his family, but he was vague and all I could think about was seeing Jamie naked.
3. All I could think about was seeing Jamie naked.

Eventually, Mum noticed I was quiet. She frowned and pursed her lips. 'You're awfully flushed, Tana,' she said, tilting my chin up and peering at me. 'Are you feeling alright?'

My cheeks burned hotter as I batted her hand away and leaned back in my chair. 'I'm fine,' I said. 'Leave me alone.'

'But why don't you want a miniature Victoria sponge? They're your favourites – you normally guzzle them down. Doesn't she, Brian?' Turning to Jamie she said, 'She usually scoffs the

46

lot, the little piggie!'

I gritted my teeth and prayed for death. 'I told you, I'm fine. I'm just not hungry.'

She tutted. 'That's the problem with the *youngsters* these days, Jamie,' she said. 'They can never make up their minds.'

After what was surely several hours of torture, Dad checked his watch, stood up, and brushed off his corduroys. Cake crumbs bounced as they hit the carpet.

I thought he and Mum were going to leave me and Jamie alone, but instead Dad said, 'Well, thanks for popping by. It was nice to meet you properly. And thanks again for looking after Tana that day.' He held Jamie's eyes. 'The silly child was horribly unwell, but it would have been much worse if you weren't old enough to drive.'

I shot Dad a glaring look, which he ignored. Smiling at Jamie, he ruffled my hair. 'She's our only baby. We're glad she didn't come to any harm.'

If Jamie realised that was a veiled threat, he didn't show it. When Dad held out his hand, Jamie stood up and shook it. He complimented Mum again on her baking. He thanked them for having him over, and said he hoped to see them again soon. They didn't reply.

I followed him outside to his car. 'Sorry about the interrogation.'

'Don't worry about it.' Jamie unlocked the door then turned to me. 'They're just looking out for you, as they should.'

'Yes, but –'

'Honestly, you're lucky to have them.'

He put his hands on my shoulders and smiled straight into my eyes, then kissed me. His lips were warm and soft, gentle, with just the right amount of pressure. Textbook.

I'll update soon!

5

It's a relief when the drugs wear off. They dig into my mind and excavate all the weird stuff going on in there. Constantly drifting in and out of sleep, where vivid dreams feel more like reliving memories, is revealing a big picture I'd been blind to. Wilful blinkering.

When I'm awake, all I think about is Meredith and whether she will come in to tell me what happened, and when I'm asleep or they drug me up, it's all about Jamie. He's patrolling my subconscious, making the situation even more confusing.

It's almost laughable how wrong you can be – about people, situations, life. The best laid plans and all that … they can seem pointless. One minute you're at school, wishing to be an adult so you can control your own life, and the next minute you're an adult, wishing you were young again so someone could give you some guidance. Is there a perfect, sweet spot, I wonder? A little chunk of time when you are free of responsibility, yet adult enough to make use of it. Do you recognise and appreciate the joy of your situation, or are these things only visible in retrospect? I can't say, because if there is such a sweet spot it never existed for me.

At sixteen I thought I knew everything, and I guess that's common. But when I reflect on my naivety, how I assumed life would pan out as I wanted and that nothing could go wrong, I cringe and wish I could go back to give myself a warning. Young Tana probably wouldn't listen though, stubborn as she was. She would say I'm boring and sound just like my parents. My plans at the time were admirable for sure, but I didn't take them seriously. Maybe I never truly believed in them.

Sometimes, after drinking a few glasses of wine and replaying conversations in my mind, I get emotional and lay all responsibility at Jamie's feet. I blame him for how my life is. It is not the right thing to do but it is easy. Being stuck in hospital is giving me plenty of time to reflect properly though, and I can see it isn't all his fault. Life is rarely that simple. Suggesting otherwise renders my decisions irrelevant, removes all my accountability, and that's a ridiculous path to walk.

My dad was right. 'You're so impulsive, Tana,' he used to say. 'When will you slow down and make some considered choices?'

At the time, I never understood what he meant. As a teenager, I assumed it was his way of having a dig at me for not dithering over everything like he and Mum did – like they still do. Going shopping with them remains a painful experience; it takes ten times longer than it should, as they discuss every item and whether it should make it into their trolley. Might they find it cheaper elsewhere? In-store reductions cause even greater consternation. Should they buy that piece of reduced Cheddar? What is the likelihood of them eating it before the use-by date? Do they really need it? They then discuss the week's menu to see whether said Cheddar (or whatever they're fussing over) might be squeezed into their plan. Is it a genuine bargain or are they being manipulated by the supermarket into spending more money?

'Did you read in yesterday's *Telegraph*, Janice, the article that said supermarkets do just that?'

'No, I must have missed that one, Brian. Hmmm. That's a quandary for sure. Do you think we need more cheese? I'll go with whatever you think.'

Oh. My. God.

When I go with them, which is rarely, I bite my lip and count to one hundred. Sometimes two.

Anyway, when all the Jamie stuff was happening and Dad had told me for the thousandth time that I needed to slow down and make considered choices, I remember shouting at him. 'Dad!' I said, 'I do make considered choices about important things! I have thoroughly considered my options and have chosen to stay on at school. Then I will go to university. That's good, isn't it?'

He raised his hand, telling me to stop yelling. 'Yes, Tana, it is,' he said, in a deliberately calm tone which annoyed me even more. 'But have you thought about what results you need to get into specific universities? Have you researched them? Do you know the institutions you're applying to?'

'No, not yet, because I have loads of time to do all that boring stuff. But because I can make up my mind in a split second about whether to have a pizza or a burger, that doesn't make me the terrible person you seem to think I am. Besides, spontaneity makes life fun.'

He raised an eyebrow (he never managed to get his as high and arched as Mum though) and shook his head, suggesting I was hopelessly slow.

'Did spontaneity make life fun when it resulted in pneumonia? I think not. Let's just hope your rashness doesn't get you into any more trouble.'

By 'rashness' he meant Jamie. However, despite their concerns about the age difference and the fact that they could not understand the point of a long-distance relationship, Mum and Dad came to like him. They even accepted that he didn't have a wife and child back in Bristol.

To be fair to Jamie, he is the kind of person who puts people at ease. He is friendly to everyone, so whenever he called and Mum or Dad answered the phone, he was polite and chatty; he gradually won them over. At the time, I didn't appreciate how much he enjoyed having parental figures to talk to, but then again, I didn't appreciate a lot of things.

I thought my parents were uptight. They acted as if doom lurked around every corner and drove me crazy with overprotectiveness. Why weren't they more like Sarah's parents, who were in their forties when we were teenagers? Mine were in their sixties. Dad was forty-seven when I was born, and Mum wasn't much younger. The story goes that I was a huge surprise, that when Mum realised that she was pregnant and not menopausal they were overjoyed.

'You're our miracle, the best shock we've ever had, the most wonderful thing to have happened to us,' they would say.

But that didn't sway me; I was embarrassed of them. They simply seemed old, more like grandparents. Still, that didn't stop me imagining what they were like at my age, because Mum was eighteen when they met, not much older than me, and I couldn't help pondering whether she had fantasised about Dad. It seemed to be all I did about Jamie. *Did she imagine him in his underwear?* I wrote in my diary. Then, *Yuk! He probably wore baggy Y-fronts!*

It was unimaginable, a young Janice in her twinset and pearls, getting hot under the collar over Dad in his suit and tie.

Their idea of a good time would probably have been a chaperoned dance in the village hall, and they expected me to be like that. But they grew up in different times. When my parents were young, life was slow. Neither of them even had a TV in the house, whereas I had one in my bedroom. I had a VCR, and a stacked stereo system which played multiple CDs. It had huge speakers. I grew up playing video games, going bowling, and to the cinema. One or two kids I knew even had mobile phones. But despite my parents living through the famous swinging sixties, I imagined all that fun and freedom was as alien to them as it was to me, in the nineties.

The way I saw it, they were dull and needed to get with the times. Jamie and I were not "courting". He would not be giving me a corsage, taking me to a dance and having me home by ten. We had a modern, long-distance relationship and they had to deal with it or lose me. That was my attitude. Focusing squarely on what made me happy, never considering the effect of my behaviour on my parents, I stormed through the summer of 1997, daring anyone to question me. Brian and Janice's concerns were just an inconvenience.

In fact, everyone other than Jamie felt like an inconvenience. He became my best friend, and I neglected all my friends, including Sarah. It hurt her deeply – I see that now.

'Tana, you're not the same person I've known all my life,' she said one day, as we sunbathed in my garden. 'You've changed so much since you met Jamie. I barely know you anymore.'

'Don't be stupid,' I said. 'Of course I'm the same person.'

'Oh yeah? Well, you've been talking about him for the last half hour. I've never even seen him, so none of what you're saying means much to me. I've got stuff I want to chat about too, you know.'

'Go on then, what do you want to talk about?' I sighed, expecting something boring.

'You're missing the point. He's dominating everything, your whole life, but you hardly even know him. How can you know him when you've only met him once?'

'That's not true,' I said. 'I've met him twice.'

'I meant when you were conscious.'

'Well anyway, we talk all the time,' I said, 'so I know him really well. I can tell him anything. You're just fed up because you haven't got a gorgeous, independent, older boyfriend. You're not going to put me off him, no matter what you say.'

She sat up and stared at me. 'Boyfriend? Who says he's your boyfriend? I bet he doesn't call himself that – you have literally no idea what he does back in Bristol. If he's as sexy as you keep saying he is, I bet he's putting it about all over the place.'

'He is not – you're jealous! Jamie and I talk all the time. He wouldn't waste his time and money calling me if he had anything else going on.'

Sarah shook her head, confusion written all over her face. 'How can you know that he's not? You might talk a lot, but that doesn't make you anything more than friends. *We* talk a lot! You are wasting your life, pining away for him, and ignoring all the boys around here. You could be having fun like you used to, instead of sitting by the phone, waiting for it to ring.'

'Listen,' I said. 'School is over, exams are done, and I have the whole summer ahead of me. I don't want to spend time with the boys around here because that's exactly what they are – boys. Jamie said he'll be coming down as often as he can, and I can't bloody wait. If I'm changing, that's a good thing. Maybe you should try it.'

Sarah jumped up from her towel, rolled it and stuffed it into her bag. 'You really should listen to yourself. See you round, Tana. Have a good summer.'

'I will.' Flopping over onto my stomach, I waited for the sound of the gate.

Afterwards, I felt bad, but was too angry and confused to phone her and apologise. *Sarah's a jealous cow*, I wrote in my diary. *I don't even like her anymore.*

Sarah didn't call me, and I didn't call her.

A few days later though I saw her, walking along the street with some girls from school. They were on the other side from me, eating ice creams and laughing, and I know Sarah saw me because she nudged one of the others who looked over. None of them waved or smiled.

I maintained my stubborn silence but a week or two later, she rang. 'I'm sorry I stormed out of your garden,' she said, 'but you were pretty rude.'

'I suppose I was,' I said. 'I'm sorry too.'

'Thing is, I'm worried about you. You're throwing yourself headfirst into Jamie's world. You're infatuated with him and it's dangerous to become too wrapped up in another person.'

The blood started pounding in my ears. 'What's the difference between this situation and any other boy I've liked?'

'Well, I was talking with Sofia and Nicole, and we all think you've lost sight of who you are. You've not been out with us all, and –'

'Because you've not invited me.'

She ignored that. 'I don't understand how you can be so into someone you've only met a couple of times. It's unnatural.'

'Here we go again,' I said, feeling my top lip curl and my fists clench. 'Play another record.'

'Tana, your mum and dad are right,' she said. 'He might be nice on the phone but the whole thing is just … well … weird! Why on earth do you want a long-distance relationship – if that's what it is? It might be one big wind-up for all you know. His friends might be putting him up to it.'

'Piss off,' I said. 'That is ridiculous.'

She was silent for a moment then said, 'You've changed so much. You've turned horrible and defensive. I don't know you anymore.'

'You keep saying that,' I said, 'but I don't understand what you mean.' My nails were digging into my palms.

'Then I will explain,' she said quietly. 'Your personality has melded with this Jamie; it's like you've conformed to his way of thinking. You're pliable and mouldable and just aren't yourself anymore.' She sniffed, as if she was crying.

A surge of heat rose in my chest. 'What are you talking about?' I almost yelled it at her. 'How can you know if my personality has melded with his, if you've never even met him? You're talking crap. I might seem different but that's only because half the time I'm thinking about him, instead of having pointless conversations about the stupid boys we know. They're immature. I'm not interested in them.'

'This is what I'm talking about,' she sobbed. 'Who are you? We've had pointless conversations about the stupid boys we know, since we were eight years old.'

'Well, I don't care what you think,' I said. 'Stop ringing me if all you're going to do is shout at me.' Then I hung up.

Stupid Sarah. What does she know about anything? I wrote in my diary. *If everyone would just get off my back, I could get on with my life in peace. I don't need them anymore.*

For the millionth time, I wonder where I'd be now and what I'd be doing if I hadn't taken Barney to Fistral Beach on that wet and windy April day. Would I have got married and had kids? Would I have become a lawyer? Would I have travelled around Southeast Asia with a backpack and some flipflops, danced at Full Moon parties, and got a dreamcatcher tattoo? The possibilities were limitless.

Would I be happier? Now that's a question. It's been a hard road, but I still love Jamie. I can't deny it any longer. In fact, I'm still *in* love with him, which is arguably worse, given the fact we don't talk. His name still tastes sweet on my tongue despite the bitterness. And, as always, whenever I think of him, I wonder how faithful he was. But I guess some things just aren't worth worrying about. Would I want to know the truth if he wasn't? Would I believe the truth that he was?

The summer of '97 was warm and, because we'd finished our exams in early June, the days and weeks stretched into infinity. Sarah kept her distance after that phone call; I don't blame her anymore, although at the time I was too angry and stubborn to back down. There was no chance of me apologising. As a result, I spent a lot of time on my own, reading my way through a pile of books in the garden, walking Barney, buying stuff I might need for the Sixth Form in September (there is no such thing as too much stationery) and talking to Jamie most nights on the phone. In a nutshell, I wasted the summer wishing he'd hurry up and come back to Newquay.

At the beginning of August, he returned. We met at the beach carpark, where I waited for twenty minutes at the gate, fearful that I was being stood up. When I heard a heavy bass beat approaching and, seconds later, his blue VW Golf with one grey door ('still saving to get that sprayed') turned in, surfboard strapped to the roof rack, relief flooded me. He tooted his horn and waved as he drove past. My stomach churned as I forced myself to walk, not sprint, to his car.

Clambering out of the driver's seat, he held his arms wide. 'Hey, how are you?'

I took a moment to drink him in: faded Levis, black T shirt, green Converse, a backwards baseball cap and a grin. Stepping into his embrace, I squeezed tight and inhaled the scent of soap and fresh laundry.

'I'm great, now. Where's your cousin?'

'We're meeting tomorrow. I wanted to spend time with you first.'

We bought takeaway fish and chips and ate on the beach, fresh out of the paper wrapping, talking incessantly as if we had not spoken in a month. Feeling that the long, lonely weeks since school ended had been worth it, my anger at Sarah subsided. I told myself she would understand, one day.

After lunch, Jamie took his board into the water and, while I watched him surf, a group of girls from the year below me at school arrived. They positioned themselves in a line, rolled out their towels and sat down to scan the waves. The prettiest one suddenly sat up straighter, shielded her eyes with one hand, and pointed at Jamie with the other.

'Do you recognise that guy?' she asked her friends. 'He is fit! I don't think I've seen him before.' She squirted a blob of sun cream onto her slim, tanned thigh and began massaging it in.

'That's unusual,' her friend replied. 'There aren't many you haven't *seen*.' She made quotation marks out of her fingers.

They all laughed but the first girl laughed loudest. 'Yeah, well, you either have great eyesight or you don't. Mine is 20/20.'

'And all the boys round here know it.'

'Bitch!' The first girl's feigned offence contrasted with her wide smile. She crossed her legs and smeared fresh lip gloss onto her already-shiny mouth. Her gaze was fixed on Jamie.

The thought that this beautiful girl in her miniscule bikini could easily steal Jamie away from under my nose caused my stomach to knot. 'He's actually *my* boyfriend,' I said loudly, 'so think about who might overhear you, before you start being all smutty.'

Five heads turned as one. The beautiful girl looked me up and down, slowly. 'That fit surfer is your boyfriend?'

'Yes.' I lifted my chin.

She smirked. 'Sure.' Looking at the others, she puffed up her cheeks and held her arms slightly away from her body. They all burst out laughing.

A slap would have hurt less. Tears pricked my eyes as I saw myself through hers – in comparison there was no comparison. The pretty girl was everything we were told by beauty magazines to be. She was perfectly petite, with shiny hair and polished nails, subtly flattering makeup and, importantly, friends. My body jiggled, courtesy of an extra ten pounds or so. My hair needed a cut. I wore an old, full swimsuit. My nose was peeling from sunburn. I was alone.

Asking myself why Jamie would spend time with me, when girls like her probably threw themselves at him all the time, I lay on my towel that afternoon hating myself and questioning everything. As I watched Jamie surf, I promised I'd lose two stone and get fit. I had to look better. I had to start taking more care of myself. Otherwise, I would lose him before I even got him.

Jamie had no faults. I was beneath him

physically, mentally, and socially, and had to improve if I wanted him to love me. Thin, attractive girls would always be able to take him away. It never crossed my mind that he might like me as I was.

By the time he emerged from the water, I had a firm plan of action. But I felt low. He would see the girls before he saw me – and I did not know what I would do if he smiled at them. I watched them watching him as he strolled up the beach, dripping with seawater, his board under one arm.

As he came closer, the beautiful girl caught my eye and smirked, then sucked in her flat stomach and leaned back on her hands so her boobs jutted forward. Her knees pointed slightly to one side, making her tiny waist appear even smaller.

Jamie walked straight past them, appearing not to notice. He stopped in front of me and grinned, then shook his wet hair, showering me with cold droplets while I screamed with delight.

'It's gorgeous in there,' he said. 'I wish you'd let me teach you to surf.'

The beautiful girl gasped, and I could have burst. Jamie held his hands out for me to hold, then pulled me to my feet. 'Let's go back to yours.'

The girl watched us pack up our bits and I smiled at her over my shoulder before we left. It was all I could do not to flip her the bird and say, 'Told you!'

Mum had invited him over for dinner. She made an enormous lasagne because she judges people by how much they eat. I suspected that Jamie never ate particularly well, living in that flat with Bradley, but after an afternoon of surfing he was ravenous, and Mum was happy to keep dishing up extras.

Too preoccupied with feeding him, she didn't notice that I ate mostly salad. It took a week or so for her to realise I was dieting (that was a whole new level of grief) but my parents, to give them credit, made an effort. The four of us sat around the table chatting and laughing, and Dad even revealed that he had enjoyed surfing when he was young. That was news to me. Later, they went to play bridge at their friends' house, leaving us alone for the first time. I think I may have lied and said we were going out too but was still surprised that they left.

It's funny, how desperate I was to lose my virginity. I pretty much threw myself at Jamie the moment the door closed. I showed no finesse or restraint whatsoever and he probably thought I was some kind of nymphomaniac – or maybe he was used to girls behaving that way.

'Are you sure, Tana?' he asked, putting his hands on my shoulders, and breaking away from my kiss. 'We don't have to. We can watch a video.'

'Are you kidding?' I said, pulling him towards my bedroom. 'I've been waiting ages for this.'

My first time was different from how I had always imagined. It wasn't embarrassing or awkward, I didn't worry that my legs looked fat or that I was doing it wrong. Besides, Jamie knew exactly what to do. He did things with his hands and mouth that I had no idea was possible ... and suddenly I knew why the world was obsessed with sex. It crossed my mind that he was an expert, but I pushed the thought away, telling myself that it probably just seemed that way because I was inexperienced. The thought of him with other girls made me want to vomit.

Afterwards we lay curled together, limbs entwined, my head snuggled against his chest. I remember looking around my room and thinking how it suddenly looked different.

'Hey, you ok?' Jamie asked. 'Are you crying? Did I hurt you?'

He tried to sit up, but I stilled him with my hand then wiped my face, embarrassed that he had felt my tears against his skin. 'No, you didn't hurt me at all. I'm just happy.'

He smiled and traced my collarbone with his finger, then gently let it run down onto my belly. 'I can make you happier.'

Those two weeks were the best I had known. We hung out together during the day and at night we would make love everywhere we found an opportunity. Jamie had a portable stereo, one of those massive ones with two tape decks that need about twelve batteries for an hour's music. We would lug it up the rocks at Towan Head as the sun was setting, so we could look out over the sea and listen to some tunes while the waves crashed below. If it got chilly, we would make a little fire. Laying back on the rocks, listening to music as the stars slowly revealed themselves, I marvelled at the fact that even though I had lived in Newquay all my life, I'd never done anything like it before.

Jamie was so different to the boys I knew. He was confident, funny, athletic, and seemed worldly to my sheltered eyes. My musical taste was limited to the pop charts, but he introduced me to a range of styles and bands I'd never heard of. He enjoyed a few beers or a joint to relax but didn't get hideously drunk. I wouldn't have any and he was fine with that; there was no question of him mocking me, like the boys at school would have. In fact, he liked that I was strong willed and had my own opinions.

We talked about everything, from kids' TV shows to the current political situations, to history, to books, to which was our favourite Spice Girl. We hashed out the arguments of the day, like Blur -v- Oasis – you know, the important stuff. Jamie was thoughtful and kind, gentle when we made love and afterwards always cuddled me for ages, making sure I was happy, or had a drink, or was warm enough. Of course, I considered him perfect. Who wouldn't?

Meanwhile I was changing. It had not

been long, but my diet was working. I started running and swimming. I had my hair cut and highlighted, and my eyebrows shaped. Sarah had accused me of being a different person but now she was right.

Mum and Dad were on my case though. They insisted on me being home by eleven every night, which was horribly unfair, but I knew there was no arguing with Dad. 'This is our house, and these are our rules,' he said. 'If you don't like it, young lady, you can go and live elsewhere.' When he put his foot down, I knew he was serious. He had his limits.

In truth, I probably would have lived elsewhere, had there been anywhere to go. If Jamie had suggested living in a dustbin with a family of rats, I would have jumped at the chance.

As the summer drew to a close, everything felt new and exciting. I was open to all possibilities. At last, I was a grown woman: confident and mature, ready for my A levels, with a boyfriend I adored.

Apart from my parents continually getting on my nerves, and the fact I had ostracised all my friends, life was great.

6

This diary is the private property of Tana Davis.
KEEP YOUR NOSE OUT!

October 2nd, 1997

Dear Diary,

I puked this morning and still feel sick. There is no energy in my entire body.

'What's wrong?' Mum asked.

'Did you poison my dinner?' I smiled, but she didn't find it funny.

She regarded me through slitted eyes, hands on hips. 'Have you been buying fried chicken from that squalid little place on the High Street again? I told you; I saw a dead fly in their window. Honestly, Tana, you mustn't frequent such establishments if they cannot even get their hygiene right.'

I assured her that I haven't been eating fast food and that it was nothing to worry about. She tutted and pursed her lips but rang school to say I wouldn't be in, and I've spent the day in bed watching TV and trying not to be sick again.

I didn't think much of it until Jamie called

his evening. When I told him, he said I should do a pregnancy test. The room began to spin.

'What are you talking about?'

'Something to rule out, don't you think?' he said.

My mouth went dry as two rogue questions flitted through my head – did he have prior experience of this situation? Was it intentional? I tried to push pregnancy aside as something to think about later, if ever, but couldn't help doing some calculations and now I feel even sicker. It's possible I am. This is a fucking nightmare. Mum and Dad will kill me twice.

I'll write an update soon.

This diary is the private property of Tana Davis.
KEEP YOUR NOSE OUT!

October 3rd, 1997

Dear Diary,

Puked again this morning, early. Luckily, Mum was still asleep. When she got up, she asked how I was feeling and I said much better, but she frowned and said I still look 'green around the gills.' What does that even mean?

I said I wasn't a fish and was perfectly fine, that I was going to school. But really, I caught a bus to Padstow. It took over an hour, but I didn't care; I had to get as far away from Newquay as possible, so there would be no chance of seeing anyone I knew. The journey made me feel even sicker – I spent the whole time with my eyes shut and my head resting on the window. An old lady sitting next to me patted my knee and asked if I was ok. It took all my effort to smile and nod, to not dissolve into tears.

Buying a pregnancy test is embarrassing when you're sixteen. Especially if you blush. In Padstow, I went into the first chemist shop I saw, which looked fine, but then I realised there were a few other customers in there and that the kits were kept behind the counter. 'Please can I have two pregnancy test kits?' I whispered to the old guy who was serving.

He leaned closer, over the counter, and cupped his hand around his ear. 'Sorry, dear, you'll have to speak up,' he said. I'm a bit deaf. Most people just hand me a prescription.'

Seriously, I'm sure that everyone else in there was watching when I asked again, but he still didn't get it. In the end I had to point at the kits on the shelf behind him and do a little mime of a rounded belly.

'Oh, you want a pregnancy test?' He didn't have to shout. He definitely didn't have to frown.

My cheeks were on fire. Nodding, I held up two fingers. 'Two, please.'

A woman wearing a pink headscarf came and stood behind me in the queue, while this guy behind the counter took about a hundred years to shuffle around, select the tests, and put them in a bag. When I paid and he handed me my change, he said over my head to the woman that it was a shame about the youngsters today.

The only place I could find with public toilets was a fast-food place that Mum would have checked for dead flies. The smell of stale cooking oil almost brought back my breakfast. Sitting on the toilet, I peed on the stick, and my fingers too because my hands were trembling.

Dread of a thin blue line is a thing, who knew? I prayed for the test to be negative, but the line appeared anyway. I cried and shook it, held it at different angles to check I wasn't imagining things, but the line stayed. It didn't care about me.

Not knowing what else to do, I walked around the town in a daze, telling myself that the test wasn't definitive, that it was dodgy. About an hour later, I found another public toilet and did the other test. Blue line hell.

The facts remain. I am sixteen, and I am pregnant.

What shall I do? My head is everywhere – I don't know what to think or feel. I don't know who to turn to or who to talk to, or what my options are. Going to the doctor is the obvious place to start, but she's bound to tell me to have an abortion and I don't want to be persuaded or forced into anything I might regret. She might

71

ask questions about Jamie. All I want is for this to go away.

There is no way I can talk to Mum because she would probably faint and then kill me when she woke up. I can't see her being helpful or sympathetic. Can I tell Sarah? No, I didn't see her all summer and we're not even in any lessons together at school anymore, so our paths don't cross. Besides, she'd probably say, 'I told you so,' and that isn't what I need right now.

Oh, why has this happened?

This diary is the private property of Tana Davis.
KEEP YOUR NOSE OUT!

October 6th, 1997
Dear Diary,
It's been four days of hell. My head is a mess.

Mum and Dad went to the cinema tonight, so I called Jamie. His opinion matters most, and I hoped he would help me decide what to do. Before I called, I imagined him saying he never wants to see me again, and that made me feel sicker, because what would I do then?

It's crazy, but I only have his name and

phone number, no address, so in theory he could vanish from my life. Then I thought he might insist on an abortion, but I don't think I want one. What if I have one and then he disappears? What if I have the baby and then he disappears? It took me ages to pluck up the courage to call but he picked up straight away.

'Hey, Tana. I've been worried about you. How are you feeling?'

I took a deep breath. 'Sick.'

'Still? That's not good.' There was a pause and then he asked quietly, 'Did you buy a test?'

'Yeah.'

He swallowed, said nothing for a few seconds. 'And?'

'I'm scared,' I whispered, tears pricking my eyes.

'Scared to take it? Or scared because you have?' I couldn't speak. 'Is it positive?' His voice dropped lower, and I heard his worry. 'Come on, Tana, don't be cryptic.'

My tears spilled as quickly as my words. I was telling myself, as much as him. 'I did two and they were both positive. I haven't called you because I thought you might hate me. I can't get my head around it, Jamie. I don't know what to do.'

Obviously, I hadn't expected him to cheer with joy, but his silence was crushing. I was sprawled across Mum and Dad's bed, and suddenly the whole room was glaring at me:

Mum's dressing table, her perfume bottles, her jewellery box, and hairbrush. Dad's slippers, all the photos of me on the walls, even the Atlantic in the distance through the window – nothing looked right. Their bedside tables and lamps, Mum's pile of books 'in waiting' and her handmade velvet curtains … everything seemed unfamiliar.

'Hate you? Why would I … oh don't cry, Tana,' Jamie said at last. 'It'll be ok. We'll sort this out.'

'How?' I wailed. 'How can we? I'm so confused, I don't know what to think or feel or do. I need you here, Jamie. I need to know what you want.'

'Ok,' he said, 'I'll come down this weekend. We can do one more test together. I do believe you but need to see it with my own eyes. It's a massive shock.'

We stayed on the phone for about half an hour, and I cried the whole time. Jamie tried to be reassuring, but it's not like my pet hamster just died. This is huge. It's major.

Thankfully, he didn't tell me to leave him alone or to get rid of it. He promised to help. But was it really a massive shock to him? Could he have done it deliberately? But why would he? We never really talked about contraception, so maybe he assumed I am on the pill. Did he know, back in the summer, that a condom had split? Maybe he just hoped it would be ok. Well, clearly something went wrong.

It's weird but I don't even think I am angry. There are so many emotions buzzing about in my body that I can't feel anything for certain. Jamie has made me feel a bit better – he says he's here for me, no matter what I want to do. He says it's entirely my choice. But does that mean he doesn't care either way?

Oh, I don't know. I don't know anything anymore. Too much is happening. And I've got a massive history essay due in next week, that I haven't even started.

KATEBRAZIER

7

The painkillers are wearing off and my mind is sharper; I remember why I'm in France.

It was a series of events that began a few weeks ago on a bleak September morning, with dark curtains, rain hammering on the porch roof, and cars hissing through puddles on the road outside.

I couldn't get out of bed.

Work was too much.

The boys were too much.

Life was too much.

Promising myself an extra five minutes, I pulled the duvet over my head and tried to think positive thoughts.

Immediately, Oliver hollered from his bedroom: 'Mum is it morning?'

Moving over to make space for his warm little body, I called back, 'Yes. Come and have a cuddle.'

'It's time to get up, Mr Ted,' I heard him tell his teddy bear. 'Let's go and see Mummy.' A moment later he gave a soul-shattering screech, then came hopping into my room, bear dangling from his fist, wailing, 'I trod on Lego!'

His pain was real – I knew that. Treading on those vicious plastic blocks is one of the most painful experiences known to humans, and a genuine hazard in my house. I should have cared. I should have commiserated. I should.

But I didn't.

'Well, that's what happens when you leave toys all over your floor, isn't it?'

Standing beside my bed, holding his foot, Oliver howled louder. 'But Mummy! It *really* hurts.'

I heard Jack's bedroom door slam against the wall. He switched on the landing light, breaking the darkness, and stomped towards my room, shouting, 'What's all the yelling about?'

Jack might only be twelve, but he is taller than me and quite well built already. He filled the doorway, with his face in shadow and pyjamas askew. 'You woke me up.'

'Oliver trod on Lego,' I said, wishing Oliver would stop snivelling.

'Oh no! Shall I call an ambulance?'

'There's no need to take that tone, Jack. You know how painful it is.'

'I know what a baby he is.'

Through hiccups and sobs Oliver told Jack to shut up, then they began bickering as only a seven-year-old and a twelve-year-old can:

'You're a drama queen.'

'You're a loser.'

'Takes one to know one, idiot.' Etc.

So tedious.

I sighed deeply, wishing I could stay in bed all day. There was no desire in me to see daylight. 'Get out of my room, both of you,' I said. 'Just get out! Go away! Leave!' They stopped trading insults and stared at me. 'Go,' I said, 'I'm serious. I don't want to hear you, and I don't want to see you, unless you are dressed and ready for school. And stop! Fucking! Arguing!'

I had never sworn at them before. They were gaping at me. Then Jack took Oliver's hand and led him out of my bedroom. 'Come on, let's get dressed.'

I burst into tears.

Maybe their quarrelling is a sibling thing, or a boy thing – I don't know because I am neither – but it is incomprehensible. I have read the parenting books and seen the TV shows, but none teach you how to deal with the constant, low-level aggravation that blows up out of nothing and drives you mad.

According to the experts, the answer to everything is to stay calm and use the naughty step, but my kids refuse. Those smug TV bods are probably just actors anyway. They probably don't even have children. They definitely don't work in a supermarket for minimum wage, and then spend the rest of their time single parenting. The only thing I'm sure of, is that the experts would never condone my methods of dealing with recalcitrant children.

By the time I got up, the boys' truce was over, and a fresh bout of arguing was distracting me from the radio. I made sandwiches, packed their lunchboxes, and emptied the dishwasher. I sprayed and wiped the surfaces, filled the washing machine and took the rubbish out, all the time wondering if similar scenarios were happening across the country – across the world. Whilst I was sure that my kids were fairly normal, Jack and Oliver's constant fighting still felt like my fault.

Although I love the very bones of them, I must admit that sometimes I hate them. Or, more accurately, hate being a parent.

There, I've said it. I find motherhood hard. Really hard. Yet parental exhaustion seems to be a dirty secret that nobody admits to. It's lonely too. I want to talk to other mums about how it sometimes feels, like I'm living on a knife edge, like I'm a failure and a terrible person. Instead, everywhere I look – television, magazines, billboard posters – I see images of perfect, happy, smiling families.

Wondering for the billionth time what was wrong with me, I felt the lows move in. These are not just mental; the lows are also a physical sensation, a pressure, a struggle for breath. I visualise them like those magnets that TV weather reporters used to slap onto their maps, remember? A thick doughy pretzel under my ribcage and a dense black cloud above my head.

One makes me feel sick, the other presses down from above.

My face hurt, my jaw ached, and a migraine threatened. Swallowing a couple of painkillers, I repeated *today will be a good day* because all the self-help books I have read say that affirmations and uplifting mantras help when you're feeling low.

Huh.

A positive mental attitude is the key to a happy life; that's what they say.

Really?

I don't believe it myself. The alleged effect of mantras is fabulously unlikely. If it were true and we can create positivity from thin air, from our thoughts, then surely everyone would be calm and stress-free. Wouldn't they? But I repeated it anyway: *today will be a good day.* Just in case.

The lows have been more frequent over the last few years. When I'm stuck in a deep hole, I see only a slice of sky – never the whole vista. When life is tumultuous, I lose the perspective to recognise a bump in the road. I hate feeling like that but, paradoxically, I find comfort in sadness. A beauty. Sadness plods along; it's stable, reliable. Happiness is frightening because I always wonder how and when it will end.

My mum thinks I need professional help. 'Tana, darling,' she had said when we talked earlier that week, 'you really ought to contact your GP. Tell her you're depressed. I'm sure she could prescribe you a pill or something.'

'I'm not depressed,' I said. 'I don't want to take pills either. I'm just stressed and worn down.'

Can I be objective about my condition though? The fact is that as much as I love my kids – please don't think I don't – they get on my nerves. It's ironic then, that right now, lying here in a hospital bed wired up to tubes and drips and machines, I would do anything to see them. I wouldn't even care if they were squabbling because that's the normality I know and the life I want to get back to. But that morning, a few weeks back, it had all got on top of me.

At 7am the postman knocked and asked me to sign for an envelope. Knowing what it was, I could barely hold the pen straight. My hands shook as I pulled out the document. Decree Absolute.

Now, I've heard that some people hold divorce parties to revel in their new-found freedom, but being officially divorced from the man I love was nothing to celebrate. My life was a shambles; I was alone, worked a dead-end job, and had no money. Even my house was a mess, and whilst that might sound inconsequential, it is always a sign of poor mental health with me. I knew that upstairs the beds were unmade, and drawers and wardrobes had their contents spilling out. I knew the bathroom floor needed a good scrub, as for some reason my boys can't aim straight, and that the sink was encrusted with dried soap and toothpaste. I knew the toilet was unflushed, with an empty roll hanging on the holder. The boys were shooting each other with toy guns, so rubber-tipped bullets would be everywhere.

I used to enjoy cleaning, but for weeks my house had looked like we had been burgled. The fact is that nowadays I prefer wine, to scrubbing.

I tucked the Decree Absolute under the pile of paperwork that lives on top of the microwave, made the boys some breakfast, and somehow herded them out of the door.

They go to different schools, so Jack walks with his friends and I drop Oliver off then go to work. The traffic was heavy that morning, and parking was a nightmare because everyone wanted to be near the school – it was still drizzling, and heaven forbid anyone's child should get wet. As soon as I found a space, Oliver was off at top speed, running down the street, weaving around parents and children, dodging little ones on scooters, jumping onto garden walls, and swinging from low branches. I followed behind with his lunch, book bag and PE kit, half envying his energy and half scanning other parents' reactions in case they thought he was a hooligan.

In the school grounds, I waited for the teachers to come out, sitting on a little bench near the playground, away from other parents –

kind of hiding away near a privet hedge. Oliver raced around with his classmates, all of them oblivious to the wet and the puddles, and the air buzzed with laughter and the exuberance of being young. For me though, it was like watching from behind glass. I contemplated the day ahead, and another evening watching television, and wished I could go home and crawl back under my covers.

Being alone, I miss having someone to share life's burdens as well as the fun. It's the companionship I miss – having your best friend by your side through winter and summer, someone who knows you better than anyone else. Things like dancing in the kitchen with Jamie, drinking wine and listening to music while we cooked dinner; laughing together at silly movies; foot massages; day trips out; celebrating our children's birthdays and achievements – they're what I miss most. The postman had delivered an end to over ten years of me and Jamie being a team and, sitting on that playground bench, I wondered if I would ever feel joy again. Imagining my future was like staring into a void.

The bell to line up startled me, then Oliver launched himself onto my lap and squeezed me so tightly that I almost choked.

'Bye, Mum,' he said, kissing my cheek then rubbing his nose against mine. 'See you later, alligator. Love you lots like Jelly Tots.'

I don't deserve so much love. Hugging him back, I said, 'Love you too, baby bear. Have a great day.'

His class line snaked its way into the school building, but I hung back until the herd of parents, buggies and toddlers thinned. With only the prospect of another day stacking supermarket shelves, there was no rush. I dawdled along, my mind elsewhere, then – no idea how – I tripped, stumbled, and fell.

Pain shot through my knees, my hands, my cheek, my chin. For a few moments I lay on the concrete in shock, gasping for breath and trying to figure out what hurt most. Then I wrapped my arms around my knees and shut my eyes, hoping all the voices were nothing to do with me.

'Are you alright? Can you look at me?'

'Here, love, let us help you.'

'Oh my God, you're bleeding!'

'Shall I get a First Aider?'

A small crowd had surrounded me. I let them help me up but shook my head at all the questions. 'I don't know what happened,' I said, holding out my raw, bloodied palms, 'but my hands are killing.'

The crowd murmured and at least four packs of baby wipes were thrust towards me.

'No, thanks, I don't need anything.'

'You need to wash your hands,' one woman said. 'Get that grit out, pronto. Go in the school toilets and run them under cold water.'

'You need a cup of tea with a few sugars,' someone else said. 'You're dead pale. I'll get Julie from the main office – she'll sort you out.'

'What did she trip on?' someone asked.

'It could've been those tree roots or that broken concrete,' said a man who was studying the ground carefully and pointing out every defect to anyone who would listen. 'I hope the school's got decent public liability insurance.'

There was no need for sugary tea, hand washing or crime scene investigation though; getting away was all I wanted. Thanking everyone, I hobbled off with aching knees and a mortified soul.

But, approaching the gates, I realised my escape route was blocked by the last people I wanted to see – the clique of four women I had nicknamed 'The Perfects' when Oliver first started school. Their daughters were in his class.

Meredith Swanson, aka 'Premier Perfect', could wear a rubbish bag and look amazing. She'd add a belt, jewellery, and a pair of high heels, and look like she was about to hit the catwalk. She had been the focus of my envy and insecurity since Oliver and her daughter, Savannah, started in reception.

Meredith was laughing, telling the other Perfects an anecdote, and animating it with her beautifully manicured hands. Her long blonde hair somehow managed to catch the light on that dull, overcast morning with absolutely no sunshine whatsoever, and I half expected it to swish in slow motion, like hair does in adverts, and for a little flash to glance off her teeth.

'Tana,' she called.

I had been avoiding eye contact but arranged my face into what I hoped was a smile and looked over at her. Meredith wiggled her fingers in a little wave and the other three turned in unison, just like the Velociraptors in *Jurassic Park*.

'Are you ok?' A small crease appeared on Meredith's flawless forehead. 'I saw you fall over.'

'Yes, I'm fine thanks,' I mumbled, praying for lightning to strike me dead.

'It must have hurt.'

'I'll live – but thanks.' My cheeks were burning almost as much as my hands. Putting my head down, I walked past them, feeling their eyes bore holes in my back. I imagined them turning to one another, eyes wide, hands clamped over open mouths, trying not to snort with laughter as they whispered snide remarks:

'That supermarket uniform!'

'I know, right? I'd refuse to wear it. Talk about drab.'

'Just like her normal clothes.'

'Don't even mention her hair.'

'Could do with some colour.'

'No wonder her husband left.'

'He's gorgeous – have you seen him?'

Flustered and stinging, I pictured myself – a

young woman who was old before her time. She wore an oversized supermarket fleece, an A-line skirt, and sensible shoes. Every item practical, and ugly. Her eyes were puffy, her face was bruised, and she wore no makeup. Her nails were bitten ragged.

Meanwhile, each of them looked like they'd strolled to school from a fashion shoot with their catalogue children. The pavement back to my car blurred as my tears welled. Before I even started the engine, they were flowing.

8

The supermarket where I work is only a ten-minute drive from Oliver's school; I could drive it with my eyes shut. That morning, though, I could barely hold the wheel because my hands were so sore, and I could hardly see through my tears. All I could think about was how I'd spend my day compared with how The Perfects would spend their day, which in my head was always as a collective and always lots of fun.

While I stacked shelves and rearranged stock, they would visit the posh coffee shop in the High Street to order pretentious drinks, unpronounceable and expensive. While I scanned customers' shopping, they would sip and gossip. While I cleared up a breakage in aisle six (no doubt something stinky, like a garlic pasta sauce), they would take a spin class, then relax in the gym's jacuzzi. Maybe they'd have a nice back massage for an extra special treat. After a spot of lunch somewhere lovely, they would go shopping, still together of course, to pick up essentials on their husbands' credit cards. You know, like the latest Jimmy Choos or maybe a diamond tennis bracelet. Meanwhile, their cleaners would be busy, making everything tidy and fragrant at home, so they did not have to lift a finger.

They had consumed my imagination; I can see that now. I was obsessed, and deluded, knowing they all lived wonderful lives. Their children were considerate, and never fought or drew on the walls. Their husbands were caring and reliable, and it went without saying that they all enjoyed fantastic sex. Their carpets did not stain; their ovens were pristine. Drippy taps, blocked toilets, flat tyres, and broken boilers never inconvenienced them, and they could all book a holiday on a whim. Concerns about paying the bills or being good mothers passed them by. Surely, they had never shoved dirty underpants into a washing machine, cleaned up sick, or bathed a dog that had rolled in fox poo? They only did wonderful things that I had no time or money for. I did stop short of believing they had bluebirds and cute bunnies to help with minor chores, but only just.

Still on autopilot, I turned into the supermarket carpark, only to be startled by a blaring car horn. The bright red BMW coming towards me skidded, its tyres screeched, and the driver waved his hand in an unmistakeable gesture. I stamped on my brakes, sending my handbag flying into the footwell, and everything spilled out. The BMW driver passed me very slowly, glaring, shouting, and gesticulating.

I finished my turn and parked across the first spaces I could find, then collapsed over the wheel and sobbed harder. The tears were for the end of my marriage, for my mental state, for being a bad mother, for my stinging injuries, and for almost being killed by a man who had then called me a fucking wanker. They were because I hate my job. Because I'm overweight. Because I'm scared.

'Tana?' Someone knocked on the window. 'Tana, are you ok? What are you doing?'

Lifting my head, I saw my colleague, Nicky. Actually, she is my friend – a good friend – and her eyes were screwed with worry.

'I'm fine,' I said. 'I just want to be left alone.'

She yanked open the driver's door. 'You are not fine! Oh, my goodness, look at the state of you! What's happened? Tell me what's wrong.'

'Nothing.'

'Don't give me that.' She leaned in to give me a hug, and I cried even harder.

'Everything is shit. My life is a pile of shit.' I rested my head on the wheel, wincing as my facial bruises connected.

'Let's get you inside.' Nicky put everything back into my bag and helped me from the car, then ushered me through the staff entrance with her arm around my back.

On the stairs we met our manager, Alan, who looks about twelve years old. He started to say something about being short staffed, but

Nicky shook her head.

He rubbed his hairless chin and coughed. 'Morning, ladies. Everything all right, Tana?'

'No, Alan, she is not all right,' Nicky said. 'I'm taking her up to the staffroom.'

He gave me a thin smile and nodded. 'Right, yes, good. Thank you, Nicky. That would be great. Keep me posted. Let me know if there is anything I can do.'

Jumping down the remaining stairs two at a time, he disappeared through the swing door into the store.

'Nob,' Nicky said, and I had to giggle.

The staffroom is somewhere I have spent enough time to know every lump and bump on every chair and sometimes that familiarity is depressing, but that morning it was comforting. Nicky made us tea, plonked herself down and opened a packet of cookies (one bonus of working in a supermarket is the constant supply of goodies in the staffroom).

'I'm early to work,' she said, dunking a double chocolate chip into her steaming mug. 'Talk.'

Once I started, the confessions flowed. Everything poured out, all the negativity holed up inside. I even mentioned my lingering feelings for Jamie. Nicky was there for me throughout our breakup and thinks I'm crazy: one day I love him, the next I hate him, I miss him, I'm angry with him, I love him again ... it's a continual cycle. She rolled her eyes but said nothing.

Explaining the frustration of dealing with the boys and their relentless arguing, I even admitted to regularly drinking too much, losing my temper, and shouting at them.

I expected her to judge me because she doesn't have kids and probably can't imagine how bad it gets, but she said, 'Yeah, I've babysat them before, remember? Those two could drive a saint to the bottle.'

'Well, they're not quite that bad,' I said, 'but, to top it all off, I fell over at school this morning.' I held out my hands and lifted my skirt over my knees to show her the cuts. 'Everything hurts.'

'You what? You fell over?' She frowned and bit her bottom lip, inspecting my injuries. 'How did that happen? Your chin is grazed too.'

'No idea; I tripped on something. I ache all over, but my pride hurts most.'

'I can imagine. It must've been embarrassing. Did anyone see?'

'Yeah. Loads of people. Including The Perfects.'

Nicky sighed. She doesn't understand why they bother me so much though, she's not the sort of person to feel insecure or intimidated. Shaking her head, she said, 'Of course they did.'

'Exactly. You get where I'm coming from. Falling over was bad enough – why did they have to see me? They'll probably laugh about it for weeks.'

The corners of her mouth twitched. She looked away and then back at me, lips twisting as if something wriggly was trying to escape. Dimples appeared on her cheeks. Clamping a hand over her mouth did not contain her giggles.

'Sorry, Tana,' she said. 'I'm so sorry you're hurt, but it is hilarious.'

Sitting back in the chair, I folded my arms across my chest. 'Oh, thanks very much. I thought you'd sympathise. You know what they're like.'

'No, I don't. I've never met them. But I know what you're like *about* them.' She leaned forwards and rubbed my arm. 'Listen, I'm genuinely sorry that you hurt yourself and I get that it was embarrassing. I'm only laughing because I can't stop picturing it.'

She pressed her lips together, trying to stop the laughter, but her shoulders were shaking. Finally, she took a deep breath, wiped her eyes, and said, 'Look, you've had a rubbish morning, but we need to do something about all these issues. It's time for change.'

'Easy for you to say.'

'Yes, it is. But you can't keep feeling this way and not doing anything about it. No action means no improvement, and if you're not improving, you're stagnating.'

'Thanks, Doctor.'

'If I were your doctor, maybe you'd take

me seriously.' She dunked another cookie into her tea and bit into it, leaving a little smear of chocolate on her lip. 'I'll help you.'

'You're adding more pressure.'

'I'm not,' she said, wiping her mouth with the back of her hand. 'I'm just saying that you're better than this. Only you can change your life, but you must really want to, or it won't happen. It's like stopping smoking, getting fit, drinking less – any ambition. All change starts somewhere. I could start with my cookie addiction.' She dunked yet another and bit it in half.

I blew out a deep breath and picked some of the gravel out of my palms, wincing at the sting. 'What can I possibly do? The divorce is final, the boys won't suddenly stop fighting, and Jamie probably moved on ages ago. He hates me. It's all too complicated.'

Nicky's eyes clouded. Her voice dropped and she spoke gently. 'It seems overwhelming now, but you can make plans. Small steps. Tiny ones, even, if small is too big. Miniscule, if tiny is too big. But moving forwards is moving forwards. Maybe start by doing something totally different which will make you feel better, like a … I don't know.' She frowned, trying to think of something. 'Like yoga, or Zumba, or … pottery lessons.'

'Pottery?' I raised my eyebrows and had to laugh. 'You and your mad ideas.'

She smiled. 'Well, maybe not that, but you know what I mean. You need something new and fun, something to get you out of the house. Break the monotony. Meet new people.' She leaned in and gave me a hug. 'Listen, I'm glad you've told me this, because now it's my mission to help. I'm here for you, one hundred percent.'

Fresh tears spilled onto my cheeks. 'Thank you. You're a good friend.'

Leading me to the sink, she bathed my hands to wash the dirt and grit out, then dried and wrapped them, and put rubber gloves over the top. 'You need to keep them clean. I'll tell Alan you're only doing light duties today. Come on, let's go back downstairs.' As she held the door open for me, her mouth twitched again. 'Imagine it wasn't you, though, Tana. Picture someone else splatting onto their face in front of their arch enemies.' Her eyes twinkled. 'It's like a movie scene – so awful that it's funny.'

I bit my lip and looked away. 'They're not exactly my arch enemies.'

'There you go,' she said, smiling.

I pictured it like she said and smirked. Then I giggled. Soon we were both laughing.

9

This diary is the private property of Tana Davis.
KEEP YOUR NOSE OUT!

November 5th, 1997

Dear Diary,

This is a nightmare. I can't decide what to do. Having an abortion would be easier, obviously, but I'd only be doing it to avoid Mum and Dad's reaction and would feel guilty forever. The worst outcome is that I'll be a single mum at seventeen and that Mum and Dad will throw me out of the house. I can't imagine how I'd cope with that and yet, at the same time, I can't even imagine it as an actual baby.

Time is running out to decide. It's already been a month, and still only Jamie knows because I'm too scared to see the doctor. What if she tells Mum or forces me to give it up for adoption?

Jamie's supportive but, really, I'm alone with this. I'm the one whose body is changing, I'm the one who lives with it every single day, and I'm the one whose head is on upside down.

It's hard to concentrate at school – I should be studying and planning my future but can't think straight.

Having kids isn't something I've given much thought to. I mean, before this. I figured it might happen when I'm much older, but I'm not one of those people who dreams of marriage and babies. Having a career has always come first. That's normal, right? Sarah always used to say she wants four kids, and I would wonder why she was even thinking about it. Four? That gives me the shivers.

Becoming a lawyer is the only thing I've ever known I want to do for sure but, if I have a baby, I won't be able to. Or could I? I've no idea. Probably not straight away but it must be possible to go to university if you have a kid. I mean, how much difference can it make? They can't be that hard to look after. Don't they just sleep?

If I have it, I will keep it. That's the only thing I know. Keeping it means telling Mum and Dad though, and that is the last conversation in the world I want to have. Jamie said he'll be here when and if I tell them, but it's still a terrifying thought. Would they even allow me to live here with a baby? I'm not sure they would. And, if they did, we'd need to sleep in another room because mine is too small for a load of baby stuff. There'd be toys everywhere.

Where would all my things go?

I don't want to take down my posters.

I don't think they'd let me live here. I think they would go berserk and kick me out. Where would I go? I could move in with Jamie, but he has a flatmate. And what if we split up?

These questions are doing my head in. When I write in here, I pray for an answer, but what if I never get one? What if I make the wrong decision?

Re-reading any entry since the beginning of October makes the choice kaleidoscope turn again, and my foggy brain gets foggier. It's so confusing – I've read some pregnancy books in the library, and they all say that being unable to think clearly is a known symptom. It often lasts for ages after the baby is born too. What bloody good is that? Why would nature make a complicated situation even worse?

Biology is stupid.

This diary is the private property of Tana Davis.
KEEP YOUR NOSE OUT!

November 20th, 1997

Dear Diary,

My life is a runaway train, moving at 100 miles an hour. I finally went to the doctor. She tutted and said I should have been more careful. Brilliant advice, thanks for that. She also told me about some pill I could have taken if I'd gone to see her after it happened. Great – but I didn't know!

Still, she organised a scan for me, and Jamie came down from Bristol. We held hands while the ultrasound woman rubbed cold jelly stuff over my belly and put the handset thing on top. Suddenly we saw a blob on the screen, a little blinking bean. She said that was its heart beating. It has been moving about all this time, and I'd had no idea.

That's when it became real. We sat there, staring at the screen, and all I could think was that another human is growing inside me. It's mind-blowing. I was crying and Jamie was too – we made our decision on the spot.

Oh my God, we're going to be parents! It's exhilarating and terrifying, but we are determined.

After the scan, we walked up and down the High Street, smiling, laughing, talking about the future, and checking the scan pictures. We couldn't look at them enough. Jamie popped into a bookshop and bought a pregnancy book, and we sat on a bench by the harbour to have a read. He flicked past the first few months then put his hand on my belly.

'It's about the size of a lemon now,' he said.

I laughed. 'It feels more like a football.'

'You look great.' He smiled into my eyes. 'Pregnancy suits you. I can't believe your parents haven't noticed.'

Sunlight glinted off the sea. A boat was chugging along the horizon. It was warm, and I lifted my chin to feel the breeze on my face. 'I've been wearing baggy sweatshirts and avoiding them.'

He laughed. 'No mean feat, with your mum and dad. How have you managed it?'

'By squirrelling myself away in my room. Homework as an excuse is not a complete lie.'

'So, when do you think we should tell them?' Jamie's voice betrayed his nerves.

The boat seemed to move faster. I turned to him. 'May as well do it today.'

'Are you serious?' His eyes were wide.

I shrugged. 'We've made our decision, haven't we? I can't see the point in waiting any longer so yeah, today. Maybe over dinner.'

'What if your dad murders me?'

'Believe me, it'd be a double homicide.' Jamie's horrified expression made me laugh. 'Don't worry,' I said, with a glibness I did not feel. 'If he gets too angry, we'll elope.'

Later, Dad looked from me to Jamie, pushing the food around our plates. 'You two are very quiet.'

I took a deep breath. 'We're fine, Dad,' I said, 'but we do have some news. I'm just not sure how to tell you.' Looking at Jamie, he gave me a tiny nod.

Dad frowned and looked at Mum, who shrugged and shook her head. 'In my experience, Tana,' he said, 'coming straight out with things is usually the best way. Is there a party, or festival or something you want permission for?'

'No. That would be nice and easy. But if you want it straight, I'll tell you straight.' I took a sip of water, put down the glass and said, 'I'm pregnant.'

Dad's eyes screwed up small. Then his face went slack, and the colour drained from his cheeks. A small 'huh' escaped his throat. Mum gasped and her cutlery clattered onto her plate. She swallowed hard and slumped slightly. Neither of them said anything. I bit my lip as the silence snarled and all the arguments I had rehearsed turned to dust in my mouth.

Mum recovered first. 'Oh Tana,' she said, her hands fluttering to her face. 'Are you sure?'

'Yes, Mum. I'm positive. I can show you pictures from the scan I had this morning.'

'Scan?' Frowning, she crossed her arms over her chest, then stared at the floor for a few moments. When she finally looked up, it was Dad she turned to. 'Scan? Brian, did you –?'

I jumped in first. 'Mum, look, I know it's not great but we –'

'Not great?' she interrupted. 'Not great?' She rubbed her face. 'That is understatement of the year. Did you hear her, Brian? Not great!' Mum's eyes were dark with confusion and her head kept moving in small, spasmodic twitches. 'You're a child, Tana – you're still at school! You're so young! What of your A levels?'

My mouth trembled as I fought back tears. 'I know – it's all I've thought about for weeks and weeks and weeks. I've been too terrified of your reaction to tell you.'

Dad's stasis ended. He stood abruptly, toppling his chair. Frowning at me, he slammed his palms onto the table making everything on it jump and rattle.

'You're a disgrace,' he said, drawing the word out with venom. 'I'm ashamed of you.' Turning to Jamie, he shook his head. 'And as for you …' He couldn't finish, just banged a clenched fist onto the table and panted heavily. Then I watched a new thought run across his face. 'This had better not get out. We'll be the talk of the Bridge club, of the whole of Newquay.'

'Not get out!' My voice sounded strangled. 'Really? How can it not get out? People will know when they see me pushing a pram, don't you think?'

'There will be no pram because you're not keeping it.' Dad narrowed his eyes and ran a hand through his thin hair. 'You can't have a baby.'

'It's not an "it", Dad, and yes, I can.' I pointed back and forth from myself to Jamie, who was staring intently at his hands. '*We* can. I've thought about everything – *we've* thought about everything – and *we* are keeping *our* baby.'

Arguing like that probably wasn't the best thing to do but they had caught me off guard; in all the versions of that conversation that I had imagined, none included Dad's killer combo of shame and blame.

My heart was pounding, I wanted to scream and cry and shout but knew that would just make their point about immaturity clearer. I had known it would be a shock and that they would be angry, but never expected them to look at me the way they did.

'This is typical of you, Tana,' Dad said. He was a caricature, with high eyebrows, a wrinkly forehead, and flaring nostrils. 'You always jump in without a safety rope, without a care for consequence. What about your A levels? What about university? That Law career you keep talking about will go straight out of the window. There will be no career. You'll have no future.' Leaning across the table towards me, he said, 'You *must* not have this baby. I demand it. You will live in poverty.'

'Um, I have a decent job, Brian.' Jamie tried, but I interrupted.

'For God's sake, Dad, what the hell are you talking about? You can't make that decision for me, for us.' I gestured towards Jamie. 'This is our situation, not yours. You can't demand anything or tell us what to do. I am old enough and I will have it.'

I turned to Mum, but she would not look at

me. Her lips were pursed, her cheeks were pale.

'Do not use blasphemous language in my house, young lady,' Dad roared, 'and don't you forget that it is *my* house. We have no room for a baby and you're still a child – our child – so yes, we can tell you what to do. You have only just turned seventeen – you can't even drive yet! How will you raise a child? Your future will be terrible. I will not allow you to bring this humiliation to our front door.'

I had no idea he could be so cruel.

'Humiliation?' Defiance was the only way to hurt him back. 'You can't stop me,' I said. 'I'm having a baby, not a lobotomy! I can still do my exams; I'm sure school will let me. University and my career can be sorted out later. It'll be fine – I'll do night school or something. It's no big deal.'

Dad's mouth dropped. Spinning around to Mum he said, 'No big deal? Can you hear her? Do you believe this child?' Breathing heavily, he clenched and stretched his fingers. He rubbed his eyebrows. His voice dropped. 'Did you hear Tana's wisdom, Janice? She suddenly knows everything.'

Mum nodded. She had sagged like a candle.

When Dad turned back to me, his eyes were hard. 'It's clear that you have not thought this through. It's nothing but one big mistake.'

'But Dad, I –'

'Don't interrupt me! You have no idea.'

He took a deep, deliberate breath. 'Babies are hard work, Tana. They're expensive, and all-encompassing. They change your life forever. Raising a child is hard enough for a married couple, let alone two people who've barely met.'

I started to speak but Dad held his hand up to stop me, then pointed at Jamie. 'You … I knew you'd be nothing but trouble.' Pacing over to the window, Dad stood with his back to us, fingers interlaced behind his head. 'A baby is a massive responsibility – the biggest there is,' he said. When he turned back to us, his eyes were glistening. Wiping them, he went over to Jamie and came right up in his face. 'Not that you seem to give a hoot about responsibilities. What were you thinking?'

Jamie blushed and looked away, not moving even though Dad's nose was rucked up like a snarling dog, and his fist was raised.

Through gritted teeth Dad said, 'I rue the day you came near our daughter.'

The whole scene was stupid – Dad would never have thrown a punch and, even if he had, Jamie wouldn't have hit him back. Stupid men and their stupid posturing. Mum was still sniffing and dabbing her eyes. They were both pathetic.

'Don't speak to Jamie like that, Dad,' I said. 'You're being rude. This isn't his fault, it's both of ours. And you're making everything worse. You can't lecture us on parenting when you're not doing a great job of it yourself.'

Dad turned and wagged his finger at me. 'Don't you dare tell me how to be a parent; you haven't got a clue. I have done everything for you from the moment you were born,' he said. 'And I don't care whose fault it is. Whichever way you look at it, it's a disaster.'

'Only because you're making it that way!' I started crying, I couldn't help it. 'It doesn't have to be. You could try being understanding. You could try to help.' I turned to Mum. 'What about you, Mum? You've not said anything for a while.'

She finally lifted her eyes, and I've never seen such sadness and disappointment rolled into one look before. 'Supportive of this, Tana?' she said, her face a mask of pain. Lowering her voice, she spoke slowly, deliberately. 'Your dad is right. You have brought shame upon us, yet you expect us to help raise your baby. That shows that you are not old enough to have it.'

I had not known that words can cause physical pain, but my heart felt stabbed. There was nothing I could say. Leaving the room, I ran upstairs, stuffed a sports bag with a bunch of random clothes and other bits that I hoped would last me a week, then went back down and stood in the dining room doorway.

'Come on, Jamie,' I said. 'We're leaving.'

He looked from my face to the bulging sports bag and back again. 'What? No, we can't leave now, we need to sort this out first.'

'Yes, we can, and we are. Come on. There's nothing to sort.'

'Tana, this isn't a good idea.' He shook his head.

'What's there to talk about?' I asked. 'They've made it clear how they feel. Come on. Let's go.'

'No. We need to stay and talk everything through.' Jamie ran his hands through his hair and looked from me to my dad.

'He's right,' Dad said.

'All you care about, Dad, is what your friends will say. So, we're leaving. We're doing this, whether you like it or not.' I looked from Dad to Mum, and both looked like strangers. 'I hate you both. I couldn't give a fuck what you think.'

Mum groaned and covered her ears. Dad raised his hand. 'Don't you ever use language –' he started, but I grabbed Jamie's hand and pulled him into the hallway. Barney barked, not sure what was happening but hoping he could come too.

'I'm so sorry, Mr and Mrs Davis,' Jamie called back to them. 'We will sort this out.'

'Don't apologise,' I said, bundling him out of the front door and slamming it shut, hard enough to crack one of the little stained-glass panels. 'Just drive away before he gets hold of me.'

'Tana, this is crazy,' Jamie said as he started

the car. 'Let's go back indoors and talk it through. They're just shocked and upset; they will calm down.'

'No. I'm not going back. I am not talking to them. They have rejected me and insulted you, so let's go. Let's drive to Bristol.'

'Bristol? Why do you want to go there?'

'Your flat is there, remember? I'll stay with you for a few days and then we'll sort something out. It'll be ok.'

Driving away, I glanced back. Dad was standing on the kerbside, hands on hips, staring after us.

10

All afternoon I've been lying here, unable to move or escape from my thoughts, but it's been strangely therapeutic. Now I can see that Decree Absolute day, when I fell over and told Nicky my troubles, is when the ball which led me to France started rolling.

I'd taken refuge in the staff toilets at work, to have another cry, and Nicky caught me. 'You can't go on like this. It's ridiculous,' she said.

'I'm fine, honestly.' I blew my nose and wiped my eyes. 'Just give me a minute.'

Nicky folded her arms. Her eyes narrowed and her mouth skewed as she watched me. 'I said I'd help you,' she said, 'and I will. But I need to figure some things out first.'

I splashed water on my face and straightened out my clothes, trying to make myself presentable for customers again, although nothing could disguise my red, puffy eyes.

'Leave it with me,' Nicky said, then turned and left.

I didn't see her again that afternoon, but in the evening the phone rang. I was making myself a cup of tea, taking care not to burn my sore hands on the hot mug, so Oliver rushed to answer it. He is always hopeful when the phone rings, that it will be Jamie. He loves to chat with his dad, which is just as well because I love to glean information from his half of the conversation. I tell myself it's not eavesdropping because Oliver speaks loudly.

He came back into the kitchen, holding the phone towards me. 'For you.'

'I've got an idea,' Nicky said, 'and before you say no or hang up, please just hear me out.'

I sighed, dreading what I was about to hear. 'If it involves water like last time you had a good idea, I'm not sure I want to.' I took my tea through to the lounge and curled onto the sofa.

'No, no aquafit classes, I promise,' she said, with a smile in her voice. 'And no roller skating either, although that was a fun afternoon and even you admitted it.'

'I did, you're right. That was one of your better ones.' Taking a sip I said, 'Go on then, let's hear your wacky plan. Skateboarding Sunday in the park? Or hiking up a mountain in Snowdonia?'

'Don't be like that, Tana. I'm totally serious about helping you feel better. I was shocked earlier, seeing you so low.'

'Sorry. I'm not ungrateful. But, knowing you, I'm expecting something impractical.'

'Yes, it probably is, but I'm going to suggest

111

it anyway. You need a holiday, and –'

She is a sweetheart but doesn't have children, so doesn't understand the impossibility of spontaneity. I laughed before she finished her sentence. 'Out of the question.'

'Don't butt in. Let me explain. I think you need to get away – completely. Away from the kids and work, time to unwind. I know you're going to say that you can't, but I honestly think you must, for your mental health. In fact, I've already asked Alan.'

'You've what?'

'I asked Alan. He said it's fine, and it's all agreed. You've got ten days' holiday left this year, so that's all ok, and I'm sure that Jamie would have the kids for you. If he can't, or won't, then I will. I'll lend you the money and you can pay me back whenever – in instalments. I've got savings.'

'Nicky, don't be crazy.' I took another sip of my tea, mostly to stop me saying something I'd regret. How dare she speak to our manager about me? Why did he even let her? Knowing she meant well though, I swallowed the angry rant that was bubbling up.

'You know I can't go on holiday. It's sweet of you to offer and I'm touched by your concern, but no, I can't. It's impossible. And my mental health is fine, thanks.'

She was silent for a few long seconds, and I realised I'd offended her.

'Why is it impossible Tana?' she asked

softly. 'Seriously, you need a break. I couldn't believe what I was seeing or hearing today. I had no idea you're so down. It will do you a world of good and the kids will be fine. In fact, it will probably do them some good too.'

'Oh, thanks. You think they need to get away from their crazy mother now, do you?'

She sighed and tutted. 'Don't be silly, you know I don't mean it in that way. But that reaction tells me that you've lost perspective.'

A tear plopped off my nose into my tea.

'You're crying again, aren't you?'

'No,' I sniffed.

Her voice was kind. 'Please think about it, Tana, because you do need a break. Spain is still warm at this time of year, and it'd be nice and quiet because the kids are all back at school. Imagine: a few good books, a nice taverna, a quiet beach. Perfect for chilling out and getting your head straight.'

I took a deep breath and looked around my lounge. It was messy and dusty and needed to be vacuumed, but I had no energy for cleaning. Just the thought of it twisted the knot in my stomach.

'Look Nicky, I don't mean to sound rude because I really appreciate the thought. I know you're only trying to help, but I honestly can't do it. Apart from the fact that I hate borrowing money, I have to get the boys sorted every day for school. I have to make their packed lunches and wash and dry their uniform, help with homework … I'm not sure that Jamie would be prepared to do all that. He never has them during a school week. Oliver has swimming lessons on Tuesdays and Jack –'

'Do you think nobody else can do those things? What are you like? Stop trying to be Wonder Woman! All you're doing is denying yourself something you need.' Her voice rose as her words tumbled out. 'Everyone needs space, and you barely get any. There are at least two people I can think of who would gladly have the boys for you and they can – believe it or not – make food, operate a washing machine, drive to the pool, and help with homework.'

'I know, but –'

'I'm not going to sit here all night trying to convince you,' Nicky said tersely, 'but I think you should think about it. The money's not an issue. The offer's there.'

'Don't be angry with me,' I said. 'I can see what you're saying and it's lovely of you, really.'

'I'm not angry. I'm frustrated.'

I rolled my eyes. 'Now you sound like my dad.'

'Go on, make a joke about it,' she said. 'But until you deal with whatever is going on in your head about Jamie, about yourself, about the boys, you'll stay miserable.'

'You're right. But it's a lot to take in and it's complicated to organise. I will think about it though. I promise,' I lied.

A couple of hours later I was watching TV, and the boys were sitting at the table doing what I thought was homework, when Jack suddenly shouted, 'What have you done?' He jumped up from his chair and loomed over his brother.

'Nothing.' Oliver's cheeks flushed and he looked at me with wide eyes, then pushed away the paper plane in front of him.

'Mum, can you tell him?' Jack's arms were wide, palms up. 'He has literally sat here, watching me write on that paper, and now he's gone and made a plane out of it.' He turned back to his brother. 'You watched me! What's wrong with you?' Oliver shrugged. Jack said, 'Mum, why didn't you stop him? You could see what he was doing and now my homework's ruined.'

'I was watching TV,' I said. 'I had no idea what he was doing.'

Snatching up the paper plane and screwing it into a ball, Jack shouted, 'God, I hate this stupid family!' His mouth twisted as he threw it at the wall. 'I can't even sit down and do my homework without him sticking his nose in. I'll have to do it all over again now – and it took me ages in the first place.' He slapped Oliver around the head. 'Idiot.'

Oliver started crying. 'Mummy, tell him not to hit me.'

A flame seared my chest as I wished again that Jamie could help with these problems. 'He's seven years old, Jack! He didn't know. Calm down,' I said. 'We'll get it sorted.'

'Why should I calm down when he's always ruining my stuff? I worked hard on that, and because he's such a baby he can't even tell a plain piece of paper from an important one.'

'Stop overreacting,' I said. 'It was a genuine mistake.'

Jack took a few steps towards me, and for a split second I thought he might hit me too. 'It's not the point though, Mum, is it?' he said. 'He ruins everything.'

'Don't say that, Jack. You know he doesn't. It was an accident.' I held my arms out to Oliver, who slid off his chair and onto my lap for a cuddle. 'He doesn't mean that,' I whispered in his ear.

'I do mean it!' Jack said. 'Besides, who are you to tell me not to overreact? That's brilliant coming from you. You're Mrs Moody – we can never tell how you're going to be – you're either singing or crying!'

He stamped his foot, like he has done ever since he was a toddler, then stomped upstairs. 'I hate it here!' he shouted. 'Ever since Dad left it's been horrible in this house. You're *always* grumpy.'

He slammed his bedroom door, and I heard a thud and glass splintering, as the framed photo of us that hung on the landing fell from the wall.

'Good!' Jack yelled. 'I *wanted* that to happen!'

Unsure what to do, I stood at the bottom of

the stairs, looking up. Oliver's little hand found its way into my trembling one and we looked at each other, wet-eyed. I wondered again how I'd managed to make such a supreme mess of everything.

'Don't cry, Mummy,' Oliver said, squeezing my hand. 'It wasn't a very nice picture.'

I cleared up the glass, put Oliver to bed, then poured a glass of Merlot. Just the smell of it made me feel better. Downing the wine like juice, I marvelled at how quickly it calmed my nerves. There was another bottle just outside the kitchen door, so I stepped out to grab it.

The door slammed shut. The key clicked in the lock. Turning around, I saw Jack in the kitchen, holding up the key between thumb and forefinger.

'What are you doing?' I asked.

We used to have a cat, and still have a cat flap in the door. Jack bent down and pushed it open; I could only see the bottom half of his face.

'Mum,' he said, 'you never listen to me so I'm locking you outside until you do. I've talked to Dad about moving in with him ... he said it is fine but that it's up to you.'

'What do you mean, I always lis – you've talked to Dad about *what?*'

Was I hearing right? Was Jack rejecting me?

'About living with him. I've asked him a few times.'

My mind was spinning – so much was

happening all at once. Rubbing my cold arms, I tried to stay calm. 'I can't believe you'd go behind my back like that. Open the door.'

'No,' Jack said. 'Not until you agree to let me live with Dad. I'll get the phone if you want, you can speak to him now.'

'I'll do no such thing. And I am not going to stand out here in the cold and the dark, discussing this with you through a cat flap.' My voice sounded high pitched, strangled. 'Open up right now.'

'No.'

'Jack, I'm not asking, I'm telling. It's freezing out here. I'm tired, and I am not having this conversation under these circumstances. Let me in.'

'No.'

Despite the chill, I went hot. Jack is stubborn and he wanted an affirmative; I knew he wouldn't give in. The temptation to kick the door and scream until he opened it was huge, but the standoff would never resolve if we both acted like spoilt toddlers. I took a long, deep breath, flexed my fingers, and counted slowly to ten, wondering when my gorgeous, happy boy had become this duplicitous, scheming, spiteful adolescent. He reminded me more and more of myself.

'Please, darling, let me in. It's cold. I haven't got any socks on, and my feet are going numb.'

'Sorry, but no. You never listen to me, Mum,

so this time you have to. You might think I'm being dramatic and you're probably right, but how else can I get your attention? I won't let you back in until you promise to let me live with Dad. Or at least think about it.'

'Why do you keep saying that? I do listen to you – all I do is listen to you boys and do what you want. This is hurtful, Jack.'

'You're making this about you, Mum, and that proves what I'm saying. It's easy to understand. I want to live at Dad's house.'

It was like seeing him properly for the first time. I couldn't breathe. 'Why?'

'Because it's horrible here. There's so much arguing. Dad's way more relaxed than you.'

'Well of course he is, he doesn't have to –' I caught myself. Deep breaths, slow and steady. I forced my voice to sound normal. 'You're right, he is more relaxed. I guess he doesn't have quite so much on his plate as I do. Lucky Dad, eh?'

I wished I could see all of Jack's face, but his eyes were still obscured by the cat flap.

'Please, Mum, I just want you to think about it. Will you?' His voice dropped lower. 'I'm really fed up with living here because you're so sad all the time. You're always having a go at me.'

The world tilted. My vision blurred and a hot spear pierced my heart. Sitting down on the wall by the door, I put my head in my hands, trying to get some oxygen. It was clear we needed to talk, but I couldn't just let him go. Not right away, while he was so disappointed in me.

'Mum?' he said. 'Are you ok?'

I looked at his chin, poking through the plastic flap. 'Please, Jack. Let me in. I promise we'll talk, but I won't do it like this. It's ridiculous.'

His chin went in, the flap swung shut and the key clicked. A moment later, he opened the door.

'Thank you,' I said, picking up the fresh Merlot bottle and pushing past him. 'Don't you ever do that again.'

'So, will you let me?' he sounded hopeful.

'Not right at the minute, no, but I'll think about it. I had no idea that you were so unhappy.' He shrugged, watching me uncork the bottle. I regarded him for a moment and noticed that his pyjama bottoms were swinging around his ankles. I'd only bought them two weeks before.

'I'm actually thinking about going away for a week or so, on my own,' I said, pouring the wine. 'You and Oliver could stay with Dad then, if he'll agree to it. How would you feel about that?'

His face lit up. 'That sounds amazing! Afterwards, can you talk to him about me living there all the time?'

'Maybe.' I took a sip. 'So, you wouldn't mind me going away by myself? You wouldn't miss me?'

'No. Why would I? You'd be home in a few days.'

After Jack went to bed, I turned off the TV and the lights and lit a candle. It was clear I was worried for no reason – Jack could not have cared less about not seeing me for a week. He probably wouldn't care if he didn't see me for a year. I finished my glass and poured another. And another. Nicky was right; I had to take action to avoid spiralling into deeper depression. A week away, a change of scenery, would do me good. It would help me get some clarity. Time away, taking stock of what was important, suddenly sounded incredible. Peace and quiet – what a luxury.

Curled into my favourite armchair, more than a bottle of Merlot down, I wrote a list of possible destinations, none too far away and none too expensive, then whittled them down to three: Barcelona, Rome, and Madrid.

A bit too drunk to decide for sure, I rang Nicky back and accepted her offer of a holiday loan, telling her I didn't deserve her friendship.

KATEBRAZIER

11

This diary is the private property of Tana Davis.
KEEP YOUR NOSE OUT!

March 21st, 1998
Dear Diary,
Sunshine is pouring through the window, and spring is here at last. Not much longer to go now until the baby arrives. I'm fat as a walrus but have super-thick hair, perfect skin, and long, strong nails. Apart from the stretch marks on my belly, it's all good.

I just wish we had our own place. Bradley wants us out. It's understandable because I was only meant to be here for a few days and it's been months, but the pressure gets to me. We're cramped in his little flat and there's no way we can raise the baby here, but finding somewhere else is proving hard. I refuse to lug a pram up millions of stairs, but the estate agents just shrug and look blank when I say that. They don't seem to understand. Still, I'm registered with all the agents around here so, hopefully, something suitable will come up soon.

Jamie wants me to go back to Newquay for a bit, to sort things out with Mum and Dad. He says it would also help him to save more money, but I've said no. I want to see Barney, but not them. I can't forgive how they treated me and the things they said, and I don't see why I should have to be the one who goes crawling back with my tail between my legs. They were the ones at fault.

'You're so stubborn,' Jamie says whenever we talk about it. 'They're good people who were just angry. Forgive and forget, move on.'

That's fine for him to say. He's not the one who was massively insulted and rejected. Mum and Dad were wrong, and they won't admit it.

Jamie rolls his eyes when I say that; he says they didn't reject me. He says I have no idea what it's like to have parents who really don't care. But just because his parents split up, had new families, and had no time for him, does not make him the leading expert on all things parent related.

His parents pushed him aside in favour of a new life and new children and he's right, I can't imagine it, but at the same time his experience doesn't invalidate mine. It doesn't invalidate my feelings either. I'm entitled to hurt and feel angry.

Mum and Dad denied both me and my baby, so it's down to them to apologise. They were rude to Jamie too, but that doesn't bother him – he says he understands why and that it doesn't matter because it was ages ago. He even calls them with updates, saying it's too important not to.

According to him, Mum and Dad want to make peace, but the last time Dad and I spoke, he said that in his day people got married when accidents happened. I mean, really? How on earth would getting married make this suddenly acceptable for them?

Obviously, I slammed the phone down and haven't spoken to him since.

'Ignore it, Tana,' Jamie said. 'We need them and their advice. We can't learn parenting from a book.'

He even had the nerve to say I should look at the situation from Mum and Dad's angle, and that I needed to grow up a bit.

I was so angry that I locked myself in the bathroom and refused to speak to him. He knocked on the door for a few minutes then gave up. I ran a bath and sat in it, crying, until my skin turned wrinkly.

When I finally came out and apologised, he wrapped his arms around me and gave me a kiss. 'I know you're hormonal and everything,' he said, but you do need to speak to them.'

'I want them to apologise, Jamie. They way they acted makes me not want to speak to them, because it's obvious that they hate me. Why else would they have reacted like that?'

Jamie dropped his arms and turned away.

He ran his hands through his hair. 'We've been through this so many times.' He said it in his overly-patient, annoyingly slow way, as if I am incapable of understanding him at a normal speed. 'They don't hate you. They love you more than anything. Build some bridges. Move on.'

I know what he is saying. But Mum and Dad don't treat me like an adult, so there's no point.

12

The nurse has been in a few times to take my blood pressure and check the machines. We smile but can't communicate more than that, so I hope Meredith comes in soon to translate. I have a million questions.

Apart from her, the only people I want to see are Jack and Oliver. Jamie too, strange as that is. We may have only just finalised our divorce, but spending time with Meredith has made me look at the world in a different way. Since I woke up here, in hospital, I've done nothing but think – and it's clear that a good many things in my life need rearranging.

When it comes to Jamie, I'm a bag of contradictions. Nicky thinks I'm crazy, says I need to move on, and I understand why she thinks that. Jamie and I were young and barely knew each other when I got pregnant with Jack, and Jamie is my only experience of love, so she is probably right. But despite all that pressure and stress, and the problems with my parents, we managed. In fact, we thrived. We had some great times. We had fun and we laughed, but when things went wrong, I blamed Jamie and accepted none of the responsibility. I pushed the lot onto him, choosing the easy option over the truth.

We moved out of Bradley's just in time for Jack's birth. Our new place was a beautiful little flat in a converted Victorian house, with high ceilings, cornicing, and original fireplaces. The windows were enormous, and the toilet had a pull chain flush – I loved all of the quirks and features. There were not too many stairs for me to manage with a buggy, it was near Jamie's work, and for the first time I had the freedom to live as I wanted. We had a perfect little home, and a perfect little family.

Life was so busy all of a sudden; I had no time for journalling anymore, but my new life was everything I never knew I needed. We threw ourselves into parenthood, learning by trial and error, loving Jack, and each other, beyond anything I had imagined possible.

The first bleary-eyed months were hard, but everyone experiences that, and the memories make me smile. Our little cocoon kept me safe and whole.

It was inevitable I guess, but after Jack was born, the one person I wanted was my mum. Flushed with birth endorphins, I rang her as soon as I got home from hospital and we cried for joy, for time wasted and for forgiveness. She became my first call for all advice and reassurance, and order was restored. I expect I drove her a bit mad with all my questions, but she never complained about them.

'Mum, help!' I'd say, as soon as she picked up the phone. 'Jack won't sleep, but the midwife said he has to nap – what shall I do?' That was a common one. I remember calling her, almost crying myself, saying, 'The books say that babies should self-soothe but I don't want to leave him because he sounds so sad when I don't pick him up.' Mostly it was, 'How do I do X?' and 'Is it ok if I do Y?'

She would laugh and say she was hardly an expert and then remind me that women have been giving birth and raising children for millennia so, ultimately, I should do whatever worked best for me and Jack. I guess I was scared that I was doing it wrong, but that did make sense.

When Jack was three weeks old, Jamie drove us back to Cornwall and we were welcomed like celebrities – Mum put blue balloons up outside the house and stuck *It's a boy!* banners across the front door and the garage door so all the neighbours would know. Suddenly, the good opinion of Newquay's aging population was not important.

One night, they even hosted their Bridge club – the very people who they had been terrified would find out I was pregnant. Mum got everyone seated around the dining room table and then called us in.

'You remember Tana, of course, and this is

Jamie, but *this...*' she scooped Jack out of my arms and displayed him, 'is baby Jack. Our little grandson. Isn't he just perfect?'

She stroked his cheek and beamed while taking him around to each member of the club. They clucked and cooed and offered me and Jamie congratulations while Jack slept on. His hands were stroked, and his head was sniffed, ('Nothing like the smell of a new-born') but he didn't stir.

I reassured the women that I was recovering from the birth very well, thank you, and had to tell the obligatory, but disappointingly straightforward, story of his arrival: at the hospital in plenty of time, six hours of labour, no medical intervention, or stitches. Mum smiled and said that Jack's birth had been easy because, biologically, I was just the right age.

I almost fell over.

It was such a lovely visit and my relationship with them changed forever. From the moment they laid eyes on Jack, my parents melted; I barely had to lift a finger the whole time we were there. If he fussed, either Mum or Dad rushed to him, rocking, changing, cuddling. Mum fed us continually, froze batches of dinner for us to take home ('Ready for whenever you need them') and they babysat so that Jamie and I could take an hour or two out to be alone. Most of those we slept. But as June was warm and sunny that year, we also took the opportunity to get out of the house without being weighed down by a huge bag of baby paraphernalia.

We walked Barney on the beach and threw sticks into the sea for him. We spread a blanket on the sand and ate a picnic lunch. It felt strange to be without Jack for those couple of hours, but he was in the best hands at home with my parents – and time away made me love him even more.

Time carried on like that – we were young, and we were happy. Jack was a pleasure. When he was two, we got married in a registry office and when he was five, Oliver was born. We bought a little house when we needed more space and although there was never a lot of money, there was enough. We took the boys down to Cornwall regularly to see my parents. Ordinary happiness.

But when things started going wrong, they went very wrong. The details are blurry but after Oliver was born nothing was quite the same – not his fault of course, but I can't pinpoint exactly why. Probably because nothing specific happened at first.

I do remember that the Christmas when he was about four was super stressful. In the weeks leading up to it, I was trying to get all the presents bought and hidden and do all the extra jobs that the holiday season brings – school nativity costumes and gifts for teachers, extra food, decorations – those kinds of things. There was so much to organise, and it crossed my mind that Jamie wasn't helping. He seemed distracted and distant.

I assumed it was because I had been complaining about all the shopping I was doing, and that the boys kept looking through store catalogues and circling all the crappy plastic toys they said they wanted, which was irritating me further. But once I had noticed he was quiet, the seed of thought germinated, grew, and bloomed. It was all I could think about, and I began imagining problems between us: he didn't fancy me anymore, he liked someone else, he wanted to take a break and was waiting for the right time to have the conversation. Funny how a rogue thought can spiral when you let it.

What I see now is that I should have just asked him if everything was ok. But I didn't. Fearful of making the situation worse by mentioning his distance, or of coming across as accusatory, I kept quiet. And, because it was Christmas time, unnecessary aggravation was the last thing I wanted, especially as the boys were so excited. I could not ruin their fun.

It was just a feeling in any event; I couldn't say exactly what was bothering me. We were still talking and everything, but Jamie seemed detached and preoccupied; he was always fiddling about with his mobile phone, and he took to staying up late after I went to bed, saying he wasn't tired and wanted to watch something on TV. He said there was a lot on at work.

Because it was worrying me, I wasn't my normal self. Some days I withdrew and other days I tried too hard; I felt off kilter and hyper-aware of our interactions, analysing conversations and searching for nuances. It continued way past Christmas, and I remember that I had a relentless internal conversation raging, where I argued with myself over something I knew could be imaginary.

One day in early February, it was just before Oliver's fifth birthday, Jamie made himself a cup of coffee. That doesn't sound like much, but it was unusual for him to not ask if I wanted one; he was always thoughtful with the little things. It upset me and felt like neglect, dramatic as it sounds. Shortly afterwards, as we passed each other on the stairs, I swear he breathed in and shrank against the wall to avoid us touching. Normally he'd seize that opportunity for a playful squeeze.

It was the final push I needed. 'What is wrong with you?' I demanded. It was not the best way to phrase my fear that he didn't love me anymore, and it came out more aggressively than intended.

'Nothing,' he said. 'I'm fine.'

He called to the boys to hurry up and put their shoes on, as it was Saturday and he was taking them swimming, and within a few minutes I was alone.

Saturday swimming was a routine I looked forward to every week, because being alone for a few hours was usually my guilty pleasure. I'd clean the house, which gave me enormous satisfaction, then sit and have a quiet cup of tea and read. But that morning while I scrubbed and vacuumed, I replayed our short exchange and analysed it for deeper meaning. What did he mean by 'fine'? Was he 'fine' because he was happy, or 'fine' because things could be better? Was 'fine' code for 'I'm in a dilemma'?

By the time Jack and Oliver raced into the kitchen a couple of hours later, ravenous and stinking of chlorine, I felt physically sick. I had thought of nothing but Jamie's behaviour the whole time they were out. Every outcome I had imagined involved him liking another woman, and the reason was always because I was not good enough. How my thoughts went from 0-60 and then turned on me, I don't know. But it happened. I was too fat, too boring, too stupid, too moany. I was just a housewife, not interesting enough for him, and the worst of it was that I had always known this, deep inside.

'Mum! Can I have a packet of crisps please?' The requests began before their swimming bags even hit the floor. 'Guess what I did? Guess who we saw? Guess what flavour Slush Puppy I chose?'

They couldn't wait to tell me everything, including how Oliver had dropped his underpants in a puddle on the changing room floor, so was currently going commando. They giggled behind their hands. The boys were their normal selves, full of energy and stories, and it was clear that they hadn't picked up on anything unusual in Jamie's behaviour; there was no atmosphere at all between the three of them.

It was just me.

As the weeks went on, my paranoia grew. On the surface, everything was ok between us, but doubt gnawed, and I felt permanently sick. I even dropped some weight but if Jamie noticed, he didn't mention it. I asked a few times if something was stressing him, if work was alright, whether I had done something to upset him, why was he being cold towards me? But he would smile blandly at a space just beside my head and say everything was fine.

A month or so later, his afternoon meetings began to occasionally run late. His backlog of work suddenly increased. He had to take clients out for dinner. One half of me was sure he was having an affair. The other half wondered if that half was being neurotic.

I was working a few shifts at the supermarket by that time; with both boys at school there was no reason for me not to be earning some extra money, and Nicky and I had become friends. Mentioning my worries to her felt like I was betraying Jamie, but I had to speak to someone.

She raised her eyebrows when I told her my fears. 'I had the impression that your family is a tight little unit. You've surprised me.'

'We are,' I said. 'Well, we were. For the last few months, it's been a struggle. I'm doing my best to keep up appearances in front of the kids, but it feels fake. Forced.'

'Do you think they know anything's up?'

I thought about it and shook my head. 'No, I don't think so. They seem normal – bickering, playfighting, generally getting on my nerves.'

She smiled. 'Well, that's good at least. But you and Jamie need to talk about it. Why don't you cook him a nice dinner, get the boys off to bed early and have a heart to heart.'

'I'm scared,' I admitted. 'What if he tells me that I'm right?'

I took her advice though – we couldn't carry on indefinitely with a herd of elephants in every room. That Friday night, I made an extra-cheesy lasagne with salad and garlic bread and packed the boys off to bed. Jamie made all the right noises as I uncorked a bottle of Tempranillo.

'What's this in aid of?' he asked, tucking in. 'Not that I'm complaining – it's delicious.'

I shrugged, acting as if were a spur-of-the-moment thing and not meticulously planned, following a counselling session with my friend. 'Just thought it would be nice to spend a bit of time together,' I said. 'It feels like I barely see you anymore.'

He forked a cherry tomato into his mouth and frowned. 'We see each other every day.'

'You know what I mean, Jamie,' I said softly. 'We don't feel ... together. And I don't know what I've done or how to fix it.' My heart was galloping, and it was a struggle to not cry.

He looked me straight in the eye and said, 'Honestly, everything is fine. You're probably just tired from working.'

We had sex that night for the first time in weeks. Afterwards, I lay awake for hours while he snored.

At work, Nicky frowned as I explained how our conversation went. She bit her bottom lip. 'He's basically saying you're imagining things.'

Something in her voice unsettled me. 'I know, right? That's what I told you before.' We were restocking the pasta from large cardboard boxes, and suddenly I had no energy. 'That's what he's been saying for months.'

She pushed a packet of fusilli onto the shelf then looked at me, hand on hip. 'I don't want to alarm you, Tana, but that is textbook gaslighting.'

'Gas what?' The macaroni packet I was holding felt as heavy as concrete, and I put it back in its cardboard box. 'What are you saying? What the hell is gaslighting?'

'Sometimes people might not realise that they're doing it but, basically, it's when a person makes someone else question their sanity, or their perception of reality. It's psychological abuse.'

I burst out laughing. 'You're serious? You honestly think that's what Jamie's doing to me?'

Nicky wasn't laughing. She shrugged. 'Well, I suppose it does sound a bit intense, but it could be, yeah. You're questioning yourself, aren't you?'

I nodded.

'And you think he's lying to you?'

I nodded again.

'Well, if he's telling you that it's all in your head while lying about seeing someone else, that's gaslighting. It's form of manipulation. Control. It's basically honesty avoidance – for you and him.'

She let this sink in while I stared at her. My eyes filled with tears, and she hugged me tight then gave my arm a rub.

'I'm sorry, Tana,' she said, 'but it is possible. You just need to find out for sure.'

13

The May half term was lovely that year, weather-wise. Jamie took a few days off work, and we had a busy week seeing friends, going to the park, riding bikes, and doing all those fun things that sunshine and time off school allow for. All the while though, Nicky's phrase was in the back of my head. *Gaslighting*.

On the Saturday, Jamie took the boys to Weston Super Mare. Without telling me. He packed up the car as if they were just going swimming, and off they went, leaving me home alone. Nothing unusual there. But it was many hours until they came home.

The boys returned exhausted and sun-bloomed, bursting with tales of the place I love to go. They told me how they skimmed stones and jumped the breaking waves. How they sat on the sand and ate ice creams. How Oliver had a donkey ride and how they wandered up the pier and bought hot, fresh doughnuts. How they played in the penny arcade and won a cupful of coppers. How Jack won a cuddly sheep from the grabber machine.

All the things I love to do.

'Why didn't you come, Mummy?' Oliver asked, throwing his arms around my waist as I stood at the sink. Looking up, he gave me a huge smile. 'We had so much fun at Beston. You would've liked the doughnuts.'

Rubbing his hair, I looked over Oliver's head to Jamie, but he didn't show any sign that he was listening.

'Oh,' I said, trying to think of an excuse and simultaneously wondering why I was protecting Jamie, 'I had to go to work today. Someone was ill, and they needed cover.'

Oliver dropped his arms and yawned. 'That's a shame,' he said. 'It was so good.' He rubbed his eyes, yawned again. 'Please come next time.'

'Yep, I will. Next time sounds perfect.' I kissed his nose. 'You know it's Weston though, right?'

'I know,' he said. 'But me and Jack think it's the best, so we call it Beston.'

My stomach twisted. 'I think it is too. Now, go and get ready for bed. You're already half asleep. I'll be up soon to tuck you in.'

When both the boys were upstairs, I glared at Jamie. 'How could you?'

He shrugged, like it was no big deal. 'It was too hot to swim in a pool. I figured Weston would be more fun.'

'But you know I love it there,' I said. 'Why didn't you come and get me? Did you really think I'd rather do housework?' My nose started stinging but I was determined not to cry.

'I don't know.' He rubbed the back of his neck. 'It's Saturday, so I thought you'd enjoy your cleaning as usual. We've already been out a lot this week. Don't get paranoid, there was no plot against you.'

Turning the tap on, I squirted washing up liquid into the sink and swished the water until it was nice and bubbly. 'Even *I'm* not sad enough to choose cleaning over a day at the beach.' The water was almost too hot to bear but it took my mind off the sickness in my stomach. 'And you saying there was no plot against me makes me think there was. I'm not being paranoid – you deliberately left me out.'

He shook his head and ran his hand through his hair. 'You're wrong.'

'So why didn't you mention it to me? Or come back for me if it was a spur of the moment thing?'

Taking a deep breath, he closed his eyes for a moment before holding my gaze. 'I don't know.'

'You're a selfish bastard.'

I shut myself in the bedroom for the rest of the evening and he slept on the sofa.

It spiralled from there. It felt as if he simply didn't like me anymore. Knowing I would be asleep already, he often came to bed late, and when we did speak our conversations centred on the boys. The way he guarded his phone however, made me believe Nicky was right.

Frantic with jealousy, I slept poorly. Bad dreams stressed me when I slept, and when I woke in the night it was hard to get back to sleep. I would lie there, wondering who he was seeing and when he got the time. It had to be someone from work. There were so many things I wanted to say to him, and I imagined the conversations, wondering what I'd do if he confessed. It was shattering. I bought sleeping tablets which sometimes worked and sometimes didn't, but he managed to sleep peacefully while my mind tormented me night after night.

When Jack and Oliver were with us, Jamie was still the loving, attentive man I fell in love with – to them. To me he was perfectly polite. But that was the issue. Who is perfectly polite to their spouse? It all felt so fake. Had he turned into a callous man, a master at covering his tracks, or had he always compartmentalised his life? I just didn't know. These were the unanswered questions which tossed and turned with me.

One morning, as the curtains gradually lightened, I watched him sleeping. The covers had been kicked to one side and Jamie lay sprawled on his back with his long legs splayed apart. Exposed. Vulnerable. I imagined slamming my fist into his unprotected crotch.

Towards the end of June, I found something

on our computer which finally reassured me that I wasn't going mad. Going through old emails and deleting the ones we no longer needed, I saw one from someone called Rose. She was Jamie's colleague from the bank, someone he had mentioned in passing once or twice, so I recognised the name. The email was work-related and not incriminating evidence of an affair, but something about her signoff felt a bit too familiar for my liking: *See you again soon, Rose*.

It had potential.

All day, I dwelt on it, knowing that whilst I have no experience of working in a bank or an office, I wouldn't have written a line like that to a colleague. Not one I had no interest in, anyway. I would probably write, 'Many thanks,' or 'Best regards.' Her tone was too casual and her little 'again' grated.

I couldn't ignore my gut feeling any longer, but the thought of confrontation was daunting, so I poured myself a glass of Merlot for courage and drank it while cooking dinner. Then I poured another and drank that while the boys ate. I figured I'd wait for Jamie and eat with him, so had one more glass.

By the time I heard the key in the lock, only the dregs were left. It was 8pm and I was drunk. When he walked into the kitchen, Jamie's tie was loose, and his top button was undone.

'You're late,' I said. 'Been with Rose, have

you?'

He blinked rapidly and frowned. He opened his mouth but said nothing. His neck flushed deep red. Turning away from me, he put his bag on the counter and hung his jacket over a chair.

'Don't even begin to deny it Jamie,' I said. 'I know all about her.' Emboldened by the wine, I took a stab at what I thought might have been happening.

'I know all about your not-so-secret lunchtime and after work trysts, so turn around and look at me. Talk.'

His face, when he did turn around, was unreadable. It had gone slack, blank. I expected more bullshit denials, more excuses about a meeting or an audit, but then his shoulders sagged, and he took a deep breath.

'Ok, I won't deny it,' he said quietly. 'I've been with Rose.' He sounded relieved.

The simple admission took my breath away and the rant that had been rattling around inside me for months collapsed. 'Why?' I asked.

'I don't know.'

'Hardly an excuse.'

'It's the truth,' he said, rubbing his hair. But he would not look at me.

My chest felt tight as I stared at my empty wine glass. 'Where have you been with her?'

'Nowhere special,' he said. 'We were just talking.'

'That might be the worst of it.'

The strange thing is that I had convinced myself he was having an affair yet, when he admitted it, the shock was still immense. Knowing something in your heart and knowing it in your head are two different beasts. Falling in love makes you susceptible to betrayal, and betrayal is like slipping on ice or tripping up a step – an ever-present risk. But you open yourself up anyway, knowing the danger is there and that it will hurt if it happens; you accept that falling in love might have terrible consequences, but you take the risk because you hope that you'll be ok, and it won't happen to you. My investment in Jamie was absolute but he still did exactly what everyone had originally predicted. I couldn't decide which of us was more of a disappointment.

For a while we were silent. All the fight and energy I'd had earlier evaporated. Feeling like my knees might give way, I sat down at the table with my face in my hands and I cried: for myself, for our sons who I could hear playing upstairs, for the shame of being wrong about him.

Jamie stayed standing. He offered no words of comfort, no excuses, no emotion at all. Eventually, he said, 'How much have you had to drink?'

I looked up, knowing I had a blotchy face and puffy eyes, and saw his nose wrinkle, just a bit. Heat flushed through me. 'I've had a glass of wine,' I said. 'What of it?'

He shrugged, looked away. 'Nothing. I just wondered. You seem a bit drunk, that's all.'

'I drank all that,' I said, flapping my hand towards the bottle. What are you going to do about it?'

'There's nothing I can do. But I'm surprised you're drinking while the boys are still up.'

I twiddled my empty glass, letting stem roll between my fingers. 'Are you going to lecture me about being a good mother?'

He didn't answer. I suddenly wanted an explosive, no-holds-barred row; I wanted to beat my fists against his chest and scream in his face and scratch him with my nails, but he wouldn't be drawn in.

'You're in no state to talk. It'll get ugly, and they'll hear everything.' He pointed to the ceiling.

'I bet you've had a beer tonight,' I said. 'Or maybe you shared a bottle of wine with Rose? So don't be a hypocrite.'

I poured the last of the wine into my glass and gulped it quickly, staring at him, challenging him to say something. A thin trickle escaped onto my cheek as I tipped too high, and I plonked the glass down harder than I'd meant to. The stem snapped; the bowl rolled over the edge of the table and shattered on the floor.

Jamie shook his head, and his top lip curled. 'Make sure you clear that up. I'm going to get the boys sorted for bed.'

Listening to his footsteps on the stairs, I wondered what to say when he came back down. In my imagination, this scene had played out in a variety of ways; like an actress I had tried it in several styles: confident, angry, scorned, a crying victim. The reality was drunk and confused. He was right that I was in no fit state to talk properly.

I tipped our cold, congealed chicken stew dinner into the bin and made myself some toast. When he came back down, I was sitting with my head propped in my hands, feeling like an imposter in my own home.

'They're in bed, if you want to go up and say goodnight,' he said.

'I will, in a minute.'

Jamie coughed and I looked up at him. 'Tana, listen to me,' he said. 'I know I've done wrong and I'm sorry. We do need to talk about it, but not tonight because you're pissed, and the boys might hear us. I don't want them to hear us arguing. I don't want them to have to go through what I went through, every night with my parents.'

'You can't wriggle out of this by playing the guilt card,' I said. 'It won't go away.'

'I know. And you're right, but please not tonight. Not while they're here. Let's talk tomorrow once they've gone to school.'

I looked at him, took in the face and body I had loved for so long. The thought that someone else had run their hands over him made the toast and wine rise in my throat.

'Just answer me one question, Jamie. How long have you been seeing her?'

He bit his lip and stared out of the window for a few moments, before giving a small shrug. 'Six or seven months, I suppose.'

I calculated quickly – since last December. So, I'd been right all along. 'And you said it was all in my mind. You're a fucking liar. Nicky said you were gaslighting me and I didn't want to believe it, but you absolutely were.'

'Nicky? What's she got to do with anything?'

'Don't change the subject; what I discuss with my friends is my business – and it's just as well I do have her because, right now, she feels like the only person I can trust. I can't trust you.' My voice sounded shrill and unfamiliar. 'And as for the boys hearing, don't you think that sleeping with someone other than their mother might be worse than hearing us row?'

He shushed me. 'Keep your voice down, Tana. This is what I didn't want to happen.'

I slammed my palms onto the tabletop, and he flinched. 'What you *didn't* want?' I bared my teeth at him. 'Well tell me then, Jamie, what was it you *did* want? Oh, that's right, one person to wash your clothes, clean your house, look after your kids, and cook your meals, and another to shag. Am I not good enough for you anymore?'

He looked away, rubbed his neck. 'It isn't like that – wasn't like that. It just happened and it was a mistake. I know that now. I love you and the boys; I don't want to lose you.'

'Ha! A mistake is something you do once, not repeatedly for seven months.'

'Tana. I know, and I'm sorry.' He stood with rounded shoulders, arms hanging limp.

I pushed my chair back from the table and stood up. 'And you think I'm supposed to just accept that? You're lying anyway; it didn't just happen. You've been lying to me for months, telling me everything is fine and that I'm imagining things. That's what narcissistic tossers do.'

'Look, we can't talk about this now, let's –'

'You can't talk your way out of this, Jamie.' I felt brave and strong – and *right*. 'I need to have this conversation now, before you think of more lies and ways to twist my words. Now I know why you're always on your phone and don't come to bed until I'm asleep – you've been having that – what's it called – phone sex, haven't you? I've heard about that.'

'Keep the volume down,' he said, his eyes wide.

'No, I won't. You're saying that all your sneaking about was by accident, and I won't have it.' I felt my fingers curling into fists, just like Jack's do when Oliver is irritating him. 'You're disgusting,' I said slowly, emphasising every syllable. 'Tell me what happened. Tell me the truth. You owe me that much.'

He ran both hands through his hair, then rubbed the back of his neck again. 'Ok,' he said, 'but only if you stop shouting. I don't want the boys to hear any of this.'

'Keeping up the pretence of Perfect Dad, eh?'

He winced. 'That's unfair.'

'Is it really? You might want to have a think about that.'

'Are you going to stop yelling?' He moved towards me, eyebrows raised, palms held upwards. 'I'll talk if you lower your voice. Take it or leave it.'

Sighing, I sat back down and folded my arms across my chest. 'Go on then.'

He pulled out the chair opposite and sat down lightly, perching on the edge as if hoping to make a quick getaway. Resting his chin on the heel of his hand, he covered his mouth and nose with his fingers, and stared at the wall beside my head. The familiarity of his thinking pose almost made me cry.

'To be honest, I'm not sure how it started,' he said after a minute or two. 'She's always been flirty with me, but I took it as a joke, as she's young and she flirts with everyone. It's just her way.'

My stomach twisted. 'How young?'

He bent forwards, picked up the glass from the floor and put the shards on my crumby toast plate.

'How young, Jamie?'

'Twenty-four.'

Bile rose in my throat. I wasn't that much older, but those years made a massive difference. As did the fact that Rose didn't have kids and all the accompanying joys, like responsibility, extra weight, and extreme tiredness.

'Last December, I went to the office Christmas party, remember? I got really drunk. She took advantage of that and started kissing me.'

I laughed without humour, feeling sorry for her for a moment. 'So, you're blaming her. None of this is your fault. Are you saying you're a victim of sexual assault?'

He frowned. 'Well now that you put it like that, probably not.'

'No, I didn't think so.' I rested my hands flat on the table and looked him in the eye. 'Do you know what you are, Jamie? You're a cliché. The Christmas party, the young secretary, the accidental kiss. How very pathetic.'

His head dropped.

I asked how one drunken kiss at a party could turn into seven months of extra-marital affair, how he could come home every day and lie to my face – lie to his sons.

'I don't know,' he said. 'I just did. She got a bit obsessed and kept threatening to tell you. I had to keep it going, to protect you.'

I leaned across and slapped him, hard across the cheek. It made a loud *crack* in the quiet kitchen and left a satisfying, vivid red handprint.

'How fucking dare you?'

He shut his eyes and pulled away out of my reach, drawing a deep, slow breath. 'Don't do that again.'

'You're a sad little man,' I said, my hand stinging. 'Obsessed with you – yeah, I bet she was. So, you had to keep shagging her, to keep her quiet. I've heard it all now.'

Wiping my eyes, I stood quickly, knocking the chair backwards, then ran from the kitchen, upstairs, two steps at a time. In our bedroom, I pulled out a duffle bag from under the bed and started throwing in his clothes and shoes. Hearing his footsteps on the stairs, I crammed in all I could and zipped it shut.

'You're making a mistake,' he said from behind me. 'Let's sort this out tomorrow.'

I wheeled around to face him, almost losing my balance as I hoisted the heavy bag onto my shoulder. He instinctively moved to catch me, but I batted his hand away.

'Keep your filthy hands off me,' I said. 'I know where they've been. And I don't want to talk about it tomorrow. I don't want to hear any more of your lies. Besides, you're in no position to lecture me about mistakes.'

He braced his arms against the doorframe, blocking my exit. 'Don't do this, Tana,' he said.

'We need to talk about it. I've said I'm sorry and I mean it. It's all over with Rose.'

'Yeah, sure,' I said. 'Get out of my way.'

He stepped aside and I lugged the bag to the top of the stairs and threw it down. 'You'd better give your slut a call,' I said, puffing with exertion, 'because you're not sleeping here tonight. And if she asks why your cheek is all red, tell her I'll gladly demonstrate on her.'

He followed me down. 'I can't do that, Tan. It's over between me and Rose. That's why I was late home – I was telling her that it must stop, that I love you and don't want to see her again.'

Nothing could have made me happier at that moment: selfish, two-faced, dick-led Jamie, being dumped by his wife and his girlfriend on the same day, and I laughed, right in his face.

'Now that's poetic justice. But if you think I'm going to change my mind, think again. I couldn't give a shit where you go.' I held the front door open and indicated the duffle. 'Take that and piss off. You can sleep in the gutter tonight, for all I care.'

He looked at me for a few long seconds, then picked it up. 'You're making a mistake,' he said again. 'We'll talk tomorrow.'

As he reversed off the driveway, I grabbed the little potted cactus which lived on windowsill beside the front door and hurled it at his car. It flew in a graceful arc, spraying soil as it soared, and thunked onto his windscreen, cracking it.

'Bull's-eye!' I yelled and slammed the door.

My legs gave way, and I slid down the wall. Drunk and numb and bewildered, with a headache brewing behind my eyes, I put my head on my knees, wrapped my arms around my shins, and rocked for I don't know how long. At some point Jack came down and sat beside me.

14

Just a few days after accepting Nicky's offer to lend me money for a holiday, I was walking past The Perfects at the school gate and overheard Meredith telling the others that she couldn't wait to go. It sounded intriguing so I stopped and retied my shoelace.

'Where's your place again?' Carly asked her. 'Is it Monte Carlo? I always forget. Probably because I'm the only person who hasn't been there.'

Meredith laughed. 'I've told you loads of times, come whenever you want. Everyone's welcome. It's in Nice – the best place in the world.'

'That's it,' Carly said. 'I get Nice and Monte Carlo mixed up. Next year I'll come; I need to experience one your famous parties for myself. Steve's parents won't mind helping him with the kids for a few days.'

'Like I said, Carls, you're welcome anytime. You all are – you know that.'

I hadn't considered the south of France, but it's still warm there in October and I knew Nice was meant to be lovely. Figuring that anywhere good enough for Meredith Swanson was good enough for me, I decided that's where I'd go. From then, everything snowballed.

Despite my assumption that he would complain, Jamie was keen to have the boys, so I booked a cheap hotel and a return flight. The plan was to spend a blissfully quiet week relaxing, reading, and getting my head together. Being spontaneous was exhilarating, and shopping for essentials was fun; most of the shops had their winter ranges in but I found a sarong and bikini on a sale rack, and few trashy novels in the charity shop. Splashing out on a red and white stripy beach bag felt like a real treat. The only things I needed were a sun lounger and a G&T.

I got more and more excited as the day approached. On the morning of departure my taxi dropped the boys at Jamie's, enroute to the airport, and even though it was early in the morning, and they had school, they were in high spirits. So much so in fact, that I had to remind myself their enthusiasm was not a kick-in-the-teeth rejection of me, but a celebration of the unusual. I kissed and hugged them goodbye, mumbled my thanks to Jamie, then sat back in the taxi, fizzing with energy.

The airport was wonderful. I relished the expectant atmosphere; it was thrilling to be alone, with nobody pestering me for food or attention. Knowing that for seven whole days I could do whatever I wanted was intoxicating – there's no other word for it.

After checking in, I wandered around Duty Free for a while and considered making impulse purchases of items I didn't need, then sat in the departure lounge sipping a latte, watching the runway, and scrutinising my fellow passengers.

Too busy amusing myself and a toddler by pulling silly faces at him, I didn't see Meredith enter. But when I looked up at the information board, there she was, standing with her back to me, looking up too. There was no mistaking that swishy hair. She read the board and checked her watch.

It had not crossed my mind when listening to her conversation about Nice that her trip was imminent. I had simply chosen to visit because she liked it. To be like her. And, if flying on the same day were not dreadful coincidence enough, I figured we must be on the same flight.

In panic, I slouched low in my chair, dug out my baseball cap and pulled the brim down to hide my face, wishing I had dressed in something better than leggings, an old hoodie, and scuffed Nikes. My stripy beach bag went straight beneath my seat. Sweaty and indecisive, I snatched up the abandoned *Guardian* from the seat beside me, held it wide, and spied on her over the top.

Like me, Meredith was alone. Unlike me, she had a Louis Vuitton bag slung over her shoulder and oversized Chanel sunglasses pushed up on her head. She wore skin-tight jeans, black high heels, and a fitted leather jacket. I guess only one of us dressed for comfort.

Reading her boarding pass as she strode through the lounge, she was oblivious to the glances she attracted. It's not just her hair, her designer accessories and long, slim legs that make Meredith look like a 1980s supermodel; she has something magnetic that I can't define. But everyone sees it. She has natural glamour, and because she doesn't wear much makeup, she never looks plastic.

As it transpired, we were not only on the same flight, but both had aisle seats, and she was seated only six or seven rows in front of me. The toilet was at the back though, so if she needed to use it, she would have to walk straight past. Wondering what her reason might be for travelling alone, I figured I would never know. It couldn't be mental-breakdown-avoidance, like mine.

About forty minutes into our flight, Meredith stood. She looked towards the back of the plane, ran her fingers through her hair, straightened her jacket, and headed for the toilet. I pulled my cap down lower and watched her heeled feet approach, but as she drew level with me, the plane hit a spectacular pocket of turbulence. Everyone gasped and then screamed.

The plane felt like it was dropping from the sky, leaving my stomach above, and I looked up to see Meredith lurch sideways, legs folding, arms windmilling. She grabbed the seat in front of me, and her fingertips turned white as she clung on.

The plane bucked and reared. Food, drink, and possessions went flying. Someone's beer splashed over my leg and a man across the aisle yelped when a rogue iPod hit him in the head. The old lady beside me magicked up a set of rosary beads and held them tight, rubbing and muttering.

The 'Fasten Seat Belts' sign flicked on, and an alarm bonged. Over the Tannoy system the captain told us calmly that the plane had simply hit several air pockets and there was nothing to worry about, but I didn't believe him, and I doubt anyone else did. People were hollering and shrieking, clutching whatever they could: each other, the seats, the little trays which fold down – but at least everyone was sitting.

Everyone except Meredith, who by this point was on her knees in the aisle; silently hanging on, eyes screwed shut, face twisted with fear. In a fleeting moment of calm, she stood again, holding her huge sunnies in place with one hand, and the chair with the other. The plane hit another pocket, which took her completely off balance; she spun around and pitched straight into my lap.

'Oh my God I'm so sorry!' she yelled.

I held Meredith around the waist, wrapping

her like a boa constrictor, holding on as we lurched up and down and side to side, screaming and praying for what felt like a lifetime. But just as suddenly as it started, the turbulence stopped. The captain announced that we were through the worst and there was a stunned silence. Then everyone cheered.

Meredith was still trembling. I let go of her once I was sure it was safe and removed my baseball cap. I couldn't exactly hide from her anymore. She stood, smoothed her hair, readjusted her sunglasses, and twisted around to face me.

'I'm so sorry,' she began. 'I –' Her words dried. 'Tana?' She frowned. 'Is that really you? What on earth are you doing here?'

'Meredith?' I said, feigning surprise. 'This is strange! What are the chances?'

'What are … why are you … this is weird,' she said, looking me up and down. 'I'm not imagining this, right? I've not banged my head on the ceiling?'

'No, you're not,' I laughed. 'It's me.'

Shaking her head as if to clear it, Meredith blinked a few times then asked why I was going to Nice during school term time. Shrugging, I said with as much nonchalance as I could muster that I was just off for a week's break. As if I do it regularly.

She nodded and tucked a strand of hair behind her ear. 'Same – I'm going to my parents' house.'

'Your parents?'

'Yeah, I'm French. I grew up in Nice,' she said. 'They still have a house there.'

'What? You're French?' But how –?'

'Hold that thought,' she said. 'I'm dying for the toilet – that's where I was going when I landed on you. Back in a sec.'

After the turbulence, having shared a near-death experience changed the mood. Strangers were chatting. The old lady pocketed her rosary beads and was laughing with the man to her left; the people in front were picking up possessions from the floor.

When Meredith returned, she stopped beside me so we could chat, and I was about to say that she was blocking the aisle when the middle-aged man sitting across from me cleared his throat.

'Excuse me, miss,' he said, tapping her arm. 'I'm happy to swap seats, if you want to talk to your friend.' He beamed at her. Meredith flashed a bright smile and thanked him, said he was a real gentleman, and you don't get many of them these days. His eyes twinkled as he said it was fine, honestly, and moved.

Her lack of surprise told me she is used to special treatment from random strangers, but I couldn't help wondering if he would have done the same for me.

I hate to admit it, but ever since Oliver

started school Meredith has been friendly; it was jealousy that had convinced me she was fake. Envy, pure and simple. Now I know that beauty does not equal bitch. I had been so in awe of her that we had never exchanged more than everyday pleasantries but, on that flight, we talked for over an hour.

Despite wanting to find flaws, I found her easy, interesting company, and we covered a range of topics. When I asked why her parents had a house in Nice, she said her family moved from there to Bristol when she was twelve.

'What was it like, moving to another country?' I asked. 'I moved from Newquay when I was a teenager, and that was hard enough.'

Meredith nodded. 'Yeah, it was. A nightmare in fact. My school in France was mixed but the one in Bristol was all girls, and some were pure evil. They bullied me for being new.'

It was hard to imagine her as a victim, but the way she pressed her lips together and studied her hands in her lap told me she was being truthful.

'There was a strict hierarchy, you know, with mean girls at the top. I barely spoke English, so they had a lot of fun with that, tricking me into swearing at teachers and stuff. They hated me, made my first year hellish.'

'That's awful,' I said, wanting to hug her because she looked so sad. 'They were jealous I reckon, because you're pretty.'

'Thanks, Tana,' she said, with a small smile. 'That's sweet of you to say. But I wasn't. They called me "straw" because I was tall and skinny. Nasty cows, they were.'

'Kids can be horrible.' It felt inadequate to say, but I was astonished by her honesty and wasn't sure what to do with it.

She took a deep breath and blew it out slowly, shaking her head. Her eyes clouded and she looked away from me, seeing schoolrooms from the past. 'Can't they just. Those girls were brutal, and I was miserable. I wanted to go home.'

'I bet you did,' I said ineffectually, trying to empathise but failing. My friendships at school were secure. Even when we fell out, I always felt safe.

She smiled sadly. 'I even tried to run away – to fly back to France. I stole my papa's credit card and made it to the airport, but they wouldn't let me fly without an adult's permission.'

'No way! What happened then?'

'Airport security rang my parents, and they came to get me.' She smiled, closed her eyes, and shook her head. 'I did loads of stupid things to try and get them to move back home, but they wouldn't.'

'Really? Like what?'

Meredith shrugged. 'Drastic measures, purely for attention.'

'What do you mean?'

She rubbed her neck. 'I should've kept my mouth shut – you'll judge me for this one.' Pulling up her sleeve, she showed me a faint scar criss-crossing her wrist. 'That night I cut myself,' she said, 'you know, to prove I was unhappy. It was completely superficial though. I only proved I was a silly child.'

My heart ached for young Meredith, so lonely and desperate that she would do something like that to try and change her parents' minds. Even in my lowest and most conflicted moments, I have never considered hurting myself.

'Wow,' I said. 'I don't know what to say. But I don't judge you. Everyone does things they regret – I'm just surprised you told me.'

'Yeah.' She smoothed her hair and studied her nails for a moment. 'But I figured you might have noticed the scar. Besides, it reminds me to live in a way that makes me happy.'

'I had no idea,' I said, wondering how my assumptions could be so wrong.

'Why would you? We've never really talked before. Anyway, it wasn't all bad – Papa kept our house in Nice and we went back whenever we could. I still see my friends when I go there.'

'It's sad that you went through all that though.' I smiled. 'Looking at you, it's hard to believe you've ever had a day of stress in your life.'

She laughed. 'You're sweet. Wrong, but

sweet. It was a horrible time, and I battled my parents constantly. They wouldn't give in though; they wanted me to learn resilience.' She rolled her eyes. 'At the time it made no sense.'

Thinking of me and my parents when I was young, I agreed.

'Anyway,' Meredith continued, 'I ignored the bullies and eventually they gave up, found a new victim. I made friends. Studied hard. I got the last laugh.'

'How's that?' I asked. 'What did you do?'

'Well, mine was a private, very academic school, and the girls who gave me a hard time were the princess type, you know – rich parents, loads of pressure, high achievers.'

I nodded, clueless, as my school was an ordinary comprehensive with stink bombs, broken chairs and graffitied textbooks. My work ethic until falling pregnant had not been the norm.

'I wiped the floor with those nasty cows,' she said. 'Got top marks in my GCSEs and my A levels.' She grinned. 'Ended up with a Psychology degree too, not that I use it.'

Another assumption shattered. But the viper of envy bit. They were my expected grades, that was my planned trajectory.

'You must have an amazing job,' I said, thinking that maybe those coffee mornings and shopping afternoons were another fantasy I'd created.

'Oh no, I don't work. Don't need to.' She grinned. 'I leave all that boring stuff to John.'

'Your husband?'

Nodding, she said, 'Yeah. He's great.'

Unable to look at her, I was glad to be distracted by a little girl in bright yellow dungarees who held her mum's hand as they made their way towards the toilets. She smiled and waved at everyone, capturing hearts all along the aisle. I was forced to swallow my resentment but changed the subject because hearing about beautiful Meredith's perfect husband was too much.

'So, how long have you lived in England then?' I asked, after smiling and wiggling my fingers at the child. 'You've got no accent at all.'

She nodded. 'I worked hard on that one. It was bully ammunition. Still, after twenty-five years it would probably have worn off anyway.'

Twenty-five plus twelve. 'You're thirty-seven?' I did the sum again to make sure. 'I had no idea you were that old.'

She laughed and raised an eyebrow. 'Please. I prefer "mature."'

Wondering what face cream she used, I said, 'I assumed you were a teenage mum, like me.'

'Were you?' It was her turn to look surprised. I guess I look older than I am.

'Yeah,' I said, 'I'm thirty in a couple of weeks. The big three oh.'

'So, is this a last hoorah for your twenties?'

I sniffed. 'Something like that.'

Meredith scanned my face through narrowed eyes, her head tilted to the side. 'You have an older son, don't you? Is he at secondary school?'

'Yes, Jack. He's twelve. I was seventeen when I had him.'

She blinked at me. 'Did you really? Goodness. That is young.' She picked some fluff off her jeans and adjusted in her seat. 'You were brave.'

My stomach flipped and my cheeks grew hot. 'Meaning?'

'A brave decision. There's no way I could've coped with a baby at seventeen.' She flicked her hair. 'At that age I was either studying in the week or clubbing at the weekend. No time for anything else.'

Maybe she didn't mean to be flippant, but her words summarised all the freedom and rites of passage which bypassed me, as I was changing nappies and doing night feeds.

'Well, I couldn't have coped without him.'

'Oh yes, of course, I didn't mean … I was just saying, for me. It's a huge thing at seventeen.'

I looked at her. 'Having a baby should be a huge thing whatever your age.'

'Absolutely.' Meredith cleared her throat and began rummaging in her bag. Pulling out a packet of boiled sweets, she offered me one, but I shook my head. We sat in silence for several minutes.

'Where are you staying in Nice?' she asked at last. When I told her, her eyes widened. 'Oh Tana, you can't stay there,' she said. 'It's a fleapit. Listen, I've got a great idea. Come and stay at my parents' house with me. We'll have fun.'

A thrill ran through me at the very thought of it. But I barely knew her. What would we do? What would we talk about? I didn't want to be indebted to her or to find myself in a situation I couldn't escape, but at the same time it would be fascinating to see her in her home environment. A case study of Meredith Swanson, Premier Perfect.

'Really?' I asked.

'Absolutely. You're more than welcome.'

'Oh, I don't know,' I said, shaking my head. 'You caught me off guard.' My chest felt tight as she watched me, waiting. 'No, I don't think so. It's nice of you to offer but I need to sort my head out. I'm not great company. I came away for solitude.'

Leaning across the aisle, she touched my arm. 'You are great company. And we all need our heads sorted. Go on, I reckon you'll be bored by Monday, all on your own. You're so used to having the boys around.'

'They're the reason I need my head sorted.'

She threw her head back and laughed. 'Well, like I said, you're welcome to stay at mine. My parents don't live there, it would just be us. We can walk into town or go to the beach, go for coffee – it'll be a laugh. You can meet my friends. It'll be much better than that other place you booked.'

'But my plan was to do lots of reading, and sunbathing, and thinking.'

'You can do all that at mine and still have fun.'

I knew our ideas of fun were different but didn't know how much. I also didn't know exactly what mine were anymore because it had been ages since I'd had any. However, I had nobody to answer to, and nobody to look after, so there was no reason not to accept.

'You're sure your parents wouldn't mind?' I asked.

Frowning, she shook her head, like I had said something ludicrous. 'Not at all. Me, my parents, and my sister take it in turns to stay there; as long as it's left clean, they don't mind who goes. They don't need to know what happens.'

Sensible Tana told me to say no. I had come away for a quiet, relaxing week to get my head straight. She said I should stay at the cheap hotel, writing diary entries and reading my books.

But Repressed Tana spoke louder. She reminded me that Meredith is fascinating, energetic, and fun. 'Live a little!' Repressed Tana said. 'What's the worst that could happen?'

15

On the drive from Nice Côte d'Azur Airport to Meredith's, everything struck me as fabulous: the bright blue sky, the warmth, and sea; even the air seemed to vibrate in a way that British air never could.

The architecture was beautiful too – every shop and café, every market, beckoned to me. Velvety petals of red, yellow, and orange exploded in riotous displays from flowerbeds, and tall palm trees swayed along the Promenade des Anglais.

With the Mediterranean on one side and gently rising hills on the other, I felt like a child at a fairground not knowing what to look at next. All I could do was look out of the taxi window and absorb the sights, smells, and sounds, until sensory overload forced me to sit back and take deep, slow breaths. The stress and anxiety I had packed in my luggage began to melt away, and we rode in comfortable silence.

After turning into the residential part of town, I shut my eyes, and by the time we drew up outside the house, I was in that semi-sleeping state that warm travel induces.

Meredith's family home was in a quiet cul-de-sac. It slumbered in a secret world, wrapped by hedges; a world where thick peace enveloped us as soon as we entered the front gate. Walking up the rosebush-lined path, cicadas and droning bees were the only sounds I heard; the only movement was the fluttering of butterflies, and just looking at the closed window shutters made me yawn.

'What do you think?' Meredith asked. 'Pretty, isn't it?'

'It's perfect,' I whispered.

We lugged our bags up the porch steps and Meredith produced a key from her pocket. She held it up, grinning. 'Here we go. Let's have some fun.'

I swallowed, suddenly feeling a bit sick. Sensible Tana said it wasn't too late to make an excuse and go to the cheap hotel, but Repressed Tana told her to shut up. The three of us followed Meredith indoors.

'Sorry it's a bit stuffy,' she said, dropping her bags and opening a window in the hallway. 'Nobody's been here for a while.' Pointing to two doors, she said, 'The kitchen is through there, and that one's a bathroom. Do what you need to – I'm going get rid of the dust. I can never settle 'til it's done.'

She went into the kitchen, and I headed straight to the little bathroom. The light above the mirror made my cheeks look pale. There were purple smudges beneath my eyes. My ponytail was saggy, and Medusa-like strands curled around my face. I told my reflection that I was in the right place, that being at Meredith's was just what I needed, but Sensible Tana muttered doubts.

After a quick freshen up, I found Meredith in the living room with a can of polish in one hand and a duster in the other, buffing the table to a shine. A sight I had never imagined before.

'Feel free to drop your stuff and get changed,' she said. 'That sweatshirt must be warm. You can sleep in my sister's room. Turn left at the top of the stairs, hers is the last door.'

Whilst changing, I debated bikini versus swimsuit. It would probably kill what remained of my self-confidence to wear a two piece in front of Goddess Meredith but, if I didn't, I would probably seem even frumpier. Trying to decide, I lay on the bed in a warm patch of sunlight, marvelling about my twist of circumstance. A week at Meredith's house! Who'd have thought it? Eventually I went for the bikini but covered it with a sarong.

By the time I went back down, Meredith had changed too; she looked about fifteen in denim shorts and a halter neck bikini top, her hair whipped up into a ponytail. Having finished her speed clean, the windows and patio doors were now wide open to the back garden, and everything smelt fresh and citrusy.

'I'm hoping you like gin and tonic,' she said. A half empty bottle stood on the counter alongside sliced lemons and limes, and what looked like two goldfish bowls full of ice and fruit.

'I do, thanks. This is a cool bottle.' Picking it up, I inspected the label. 'Citadelle. Such a pretty blue.'

'Nice, right? It's a French one – delicious too.' She handed me a goldfish bowl, clinked hers against mine and said, 'Cheers. Here's to a fun week.'

'To a fun week,' I echoed. Taking a sip made my eyes water. 'It's strong!' I coughed. Thanks for having me, I really appreciate it – but I'm not sure I'll be able to drink all this.'

'Yeah, you will,' she laughed. She sipped hers and the ice cubes rattled. 'Now, let's put some tunes on and go sunbathe.'

We chose a Bob Marley CD, and I followed Meredith down the path to a kidney-shaped swimming pool. Sunshine sparkled on the water. The patio area had a table and chairs, a chiminea, and a built-in barbeque. The air hung heavy with scent from the rosebushes, which flickered with butterflies and bees. I relaxed onto a lounger, shut my eyes and breathed deeply. Music played, and heat penetrated my skin.

'Do you want another, Tana?'

Only ice remained in Meredith's glass. 'You made short work of that!'

'Years of practice,' she said, with a grin. 'So, do you want one or not?'

I downed the rest of mine and handed her the empty glass. 'Go on then. Thanks.'

While Meredith made her way back to the house, I studied her closely – looking for defects, if I'm honest. There were none. She may as well have been made in a factory. To look like her and to have this life … it wasn't fair.

The music stopped. I moved to the edge of the pool and dangled my legs in, leaned back on my hands and lifted my face to the sky. It was turquoise, broken only by a few wispy clouds and a dissipating vapour trail, the responsible plane just a tiny speck. Wrapped in warmth and quiet, with a nice alcohol buzz, there was nowhere else I would rather have been at that moment. Thinking briefly about England, I smiled, assuming it would be raining there. I kicked my feet in the cool water and waited for Meredith.

The peace was suddenly shattered by Girls Aloud, the volume cranked. My first thought was that if I lived next door I would complain, but I pushed it aside and decided it was fun to be on the rowdy side of the fence for a change. It felt rebellious.

Meredith sashayed back down the path carrying fresh drinks. Her eyes were glittery. 'Sorry I was so long,' she said, with a wide smile. 'I just called my friends – you know, the ones I was telling you about. They're coming over in a bit. We'll all go to a local bar tonight, if that's ok with you?' She handed me my glass, sniffed, and rubbed her nose. 'Sorry to just assume you'd be up for it – I mean you don't have to if you don't want to – but I thought you might like to hang out. It'll be fun for you to meet them all.'

My heart sank. I'd packed lightly, assuming I would only see the beach, the markets and maybe a little taverna. No fancy clothes. Borrowing any of Meredith's was out of the question because my arm wouldn't fit into a leg of her jeans. Saying no was rude and unsociable, but having nothing nice to wear was plain embarrassing. My mind rummaged through my suitcase, trying to find something – anything – appropriate.

Meredith didn't notice. She was feverish with excitement, twittering on and on about her friends and the fun we would have and how much I would love them. Sniffing again, she said, 'So, what do you think? Will you come out with us?'

'Are you ok?' I asked. 'Are you coming down with a cold?'

She frowned and then laughed. 'Oh, no, I'm fine. Ab-so-lute-ly fine. It's just the dust and polish.' Holding her hand out, she said, 'Come on, this is a great tune. Let's have a boogie.'

I shook my head, wanting to crawl away and hide, but she shrugged, said, 'Suit yourself,' and started dancing around the edge of the pool. With a cigarette in one hand and her drink in the other, she sang along to "Love Machine", badly and loudly, but having fun with or without me.

I watched her, willing myself to stay put, but her happiness was infectious; I kicked my feet in the water and wiggled on my backside, mouthing the lyrics. Avoidance was not an option though. As she twisted near, she grabbed my arm and pulled.

'Come on! Get up!' she shouted. 'It's "The Promise," it's the law to dance!'

Meredith sang louder, waving her arms and moving her feet with the beat. She moved without effort, and I tried to copy but it was hard – she was supple, while my limbs were sluggish and clumsy, and my thighs were jiggly.

'Feel the bassline,' she said, clasping my hands and moving me. 'Sway with the rhythm. Shake your backside.'

She was so fluid that I had to laugh at my poor imitation, but followed her lead anyway, figuring that the whole situation was so absurd I may as well go along with it. With drinks in hand in the sunshine, we danced around the pool, singing along even when we didn't know the words. The fact that we had no school run that afternoon made every moment better.

The gin melted my inhibitions and time took on a strange, elastic quality; it seemed to expand and contract rather than plod along steadily. The heat and the booze, the loud music, and the novelty of being away from home played tricks on my mind. It felt like we had been friends forever, as we held hands and danced.

'You know,' I shouted, over a song I hadn't heard before, 'I call you and your friends The Perfects.'

The music ended abruptly, leaving my words hanging in the air. I wished I could pull them down and bury them. Meredith stopped dancing. With hands on hips, panting heavily, she stared at me. And sniffed.

'Why on earth would you do that?'

My chest, neck and face went hot as I tried to think straight. 'Oh, I don't know – forget it. I shouldn't have said anything.'

'No, seriously, I want to know.' She rubbed her nose. 'The Perfects. What does that even mean?' Picking up our empty glasses, she stalked away up the path towards the house.

Sometimes, speaking your truth is a great idea. Other times, it isn't. Meredith is far from stupid, and it was obvious that I hadn't been joking. She was not going to let it go. Having turned the music down, she returned with fresh drinks and sat on the edge of her sun lounger, looking at me expectantly.

'Go on then – let's hear it.'

It was hard to tell whether she was angry, amused, intrigued, or insulted, but she was waiting for me to explain. I debated lying but was too tipsy to come up with anything even half resembling a convincing justification. In any event, the need to tell her swamped me. So, I did.

'You and your friends make me feel inadequate.'

Her brows arched, then dipped. She tilted her head and studied me. 'Inadequate? Surely that's something you do to yourself. Please explain what you mean.' She sniffed and rubbed her nose again.

I bit my lip, wishing we had not been on the same flight. It was clear I couldn't wangle my way out of the conversation though, so I figured I should just be honest. In for a penny, and all that. At first, what I said didn't make much sense – even to me – but the longer I talked, the clearer my tangled web of envy and admiration became. Like pulling a thread, my melancholy and insecurity unravelled, and Meredith just listened: head tilted, lips pursed, forehead creased.

It could have been her sympathetic reaction that made me see how much I had blown it out of proportion, or it could have been the curious effect that confession can have on deep, dark thoughts, but saying aloud what had seemed so huge for so long in my head, diminished my fears into something entirely manageable as soon as they reached the air. I could not stress enough how long I had felt that way, how envious I was of Meredith and her friends, how perfect I believed them and their lives to be.

They had become a ridiculous fantasy, that was obvious, but while articulating how inadequate I felt in comparison, I finally heard myself. While I talked, the feelings that had sent me into fits of self-loathing at worst and onto fad diets at best, shrank. Not only that but she shrank too, from deity to mortal.

The best thing about unburdening was the liberation I felt, when I recognised the absurdity of channelling my insecurities onto people I don't even know. Meredith was right – she and her friends had done nothing to me. I had done it to myself.

When I finally finished, her face was blank. After draining the rest of her drink, she lit a menthol cigarette and drew on it deeply, blowing the smoke out through her nose.

I shrugged. 'Well, you wanted to know.'

'Can't say I was expecting that,' she said at last, slowly shaking her head. 'Of course, it's flattering to hear you say all those nice things – but honestly, Tana, you have no idea how wrong you are. You are *so* wrong. Crazy wrong.' She sniffed. 'I'm a mess, not someone to admire.'

'Don't be silly, of course you're –'

'I'm serious. You're way off the mark.'

The moment popped like a bubble as five people came through the side gate calling Meredith's name. She squealed, clapped her hands, then jumped up and ran to meet them.

I watched the friends hugging and kissing, laughing, and talking all at once, and their love roused my green-eyed monster again. Meredith is lucky, no matter what she thinks of herself. She has friends and is clever and beautiful and popular. She enjoys family and freedom. I couldn't understand why she would describe herself as a mess.

Knowing I didn't belong, I decided to get my things from upstairs and make a swift exit. The fleapit hotel would be fine.

'Tana!' Meredith called, beckoning me over. 'Come and meet everyone.'

All eyes were on me as I walked over, half naked, sunburned, and drunk. Meredith was standing beside a tall man with short, dark hair and a stubbly beard; she had one arm around his waist and the other resting on his stomach.

'This is Marco,' she said, smiling up at him. Then she pointed to the others in turn. 'And this is Stefan, Amélie, Céleste and Ella.'

We smiled and said our *bonjours*, but their English was about as good as my French. Feeling like a raspberry on a blackberry bush, I told Meredith of my plan to leave, but she wouldn't hear of it and insisted that I stay for dinner, go out with them later ('It's Friday night, after all!') and make up my mind the next day. Arguing that I would spoil their fun just made her laugh and say I worry too much.

To be fair, it was nice eating together in

her kitchen, and the pasta and pesto dish she made was a triumph, washed down with several bottles of red wine. Later, we walked to a local bar for cocktails and got comfortable on the leather sofas in the corner.

Drinking to excess improved communication somehow and, as the night wore on, Stefan became more and more attractive. His blue eyes were kind and twinkly, his full lips inviting. Continually asking Meredith to translate for him, or explain the jokes, Stefan kept me included and made sure my glass did not stay empty for long; every time he passed me a drink I caught a whiff of his aftershave, clean and spicy.

At first, I thought I was imagining his attentiveness, but then realised it was because I hadn't experienced anything like it for a long time. He was flirting. Repressed Tana piped up: *He is lovely, and he likes you. Live a little.*

Sensible Tana reminded me that I did not know him at all.

Towards closing time, when I was seeing double and wishing for my bed, it crossed my mind that everyone else still seemed bright-eyed and energetic. Wondering how that could be, I noticed Stefan lean towards Meredith and whisper in her ear. She glanced at me and shook her head. He shrugged, then saw me watching and winked.

'What was that about?' I asked, but

Meredith told me it was nothing – just Stefan being Stefan. Too drunk to think about it more, I closed my eyes and let the room spin.

16

The next morning, I awoke to sunshine pouring through the window. Baking in sweaty sheets, with a brass band marching through my head and a swollen, parched tongue, I could not remember getting home, but could remember telling Meredith about 'The Perfects'.

Death seemed preferable.

Groaning, I rolled over. The room tilted, vomit rose in my throat, and I clung to the mattress, berating myself. The quiet week of soul-searching and relaxation I had planned had, so far, delivered only a hangover and humiliation.

Jack and Oliver wandered into my mind, with bag loads of guilt. Yesterday, while behaving like a teenager, I had not given them much thought. Now I questioned what kind of mother abandons her children, just to get plastered and pass out in the company of strangers?

France was a mistake; that much was clear. I should have refused Nicky's offer – I should have said that it was kind, but impossible. Figuring that Meredith might want me to leave, I resolved again to relocate to the cheap hotel, get my original plans back on track, then call the boys. Meredith's lifestyle was incongruous with mine and it was imperative that I should have the week I planned. But first I needed water and painkillers.

Downstairs, the kitchen stank of cigarettes and alcohol. A smoky grey fog hung in the air. The countertop was covered with the detritus of an after-bar party I had no recollection of attending: overflowing ash trays, empty wine bottles, three empty gin bottles, dirty plates and glasses, the claggy remains of Meredith's pasta. There were lighters, lipsticks, money, keys, and credit cards – even a dusty mirror lay on the table, and I wondered what level of vanity would prompt someone to check their appearance after a heavy night of drinking.

After swallowing two aspirins with a pint of water, I put the kettle on, opened the garden door to air the room, and began clearing up. As I washed and wiped and scrubbed and stacked, the nausea gradually eased, and my head throbbed less. I just had to avoid all sudden, jerky movements.

An hour later, the kitchen was clean, and I was sipping a coffee when the three girls padded in, pale and bleary-eyed. Céleste was rubbing her forehead and groaning; she accepted the painkillers I offered with a grateful smile and a hoarse, '*Merci*.'

Amélie raided the fridge, then she and Ella began cooking a feast of toast, coffee, eggs, bacon, and pancakes. The smells must have wafted upstairs because within minutes I heard footsteps, and Meredith came in with Marco right behind. Even with tousled hair and the declaration of a raging hangover, she looked beautiful.

'Morning, Tana,' she said, yawning. 'How are you feeling?'

I grimaced. 'Pretty rough to be honest.'

'Me too. Never mind, you'll feel fine after eating.'

As she spoke, Marco draped his arm over her shoulder and dropped a gentle kiss onto the back of her neck. She smiled, twisted into him, and placed her palm on his chest. Lifting her face, they kissed.

I turned away quickly. Was I stupid? Did going away on your own mean a love affair? Had Meredith and Marco behaved like a couple when we were in the bar? I couldn't recall anything obvious.

Needing a distraction, I reached for a glass of orange juice, but just then Stefan came in, pulling on a T shirt. The sight of his tanned, flat belly with well-defined abs flustered me, and I knocked the glass over, spilling juice across the counter. It ran and dripped onto my freshly mopped floor.

'Sorry,' I mumbled, grabbing a handful of

napkins, and dabbing the puddle. 'I'm so clumsy.'

'Don't worry about it.' Meredith unwrapped herself from Marco and passed me a tea towel, which darkened when I spread it over the spillage.

Heat flushed through me. My hands were shaking, my heart was pounding, and I felt dizzy. 'I didn't know about you and Marco,' I said. I couldn't look at her. 'Not that it's any of my business of course. It just took me by surprise, that's all.'

Meredith didn't answer. She poured a coffee and lit a cigarette, drawing deeply before blowing smoke rings towards the open door.

'Sorry. I meant to say something but forgot. We've been friends forever, as you know; he and I always hook up when I come back. We have done since we were teenagers.' She shrugged. 'We have a few mad weekends together a year … it doesn't mean anything.'

'You don't have to justify it.' I kept scrubbing at the floor, working the spot until no stickiness remained, all the time wondering how to behave.

'It's dry, leave it, it's fine,' Meredith said. 'Besides, breakfast is ready. Grab a plate, Tana. Help yourself.'

'Thanks.' I stood and surveyed the mountain of food the girls had whipped up. 'Please tell them it looks amazing.' I still could not make eye contact with her. Meredith laughed and I assumed my discomfort was evident.

'Look, get your breakfast, and come and sit outside. I'll try to explain.'

Suddenly starving, I loaded a plate with toast and eggs, and took a seat in the sunshine. Willing my voice to sound normal, I asked, 'So, what about your husband?' It felt important to know.

Meredith sipped her coffee. 'John knows. Obviously, it's not something we discuss directly, but me and Marco are a kind of unspoken agreement. John's quite a bit older than me, you see, and he knew about it from the start.'

I didn't see. My brain was throwing up all sorts of questions and I knew they'd start spilling without a filter. Regardless of her husband's age, she was betraying him, and I couldn't comprehend how she could see it any other way. Everyone is different, I realise that, but I've always assumed that other people see the world pretty much as I do, because they live in the same area, or are a similar age, or because our kids go to the same school. How ignorant could I be? Had I been living with curtains drawn across my eyes?

If I had, Meredith was twitching them open, showing me other perspectives, yet her life choices astonished me. She had said she was a mess, but we never finished the conversation; it occurred to me that she must have been referring to her unusual marriage, the Marco situation, and her excessive drinking.

'How much older is John, and how does it make a difference? What is he, like eighty?'

She rolled her eyes. 'No, of course he's not that old – but his age does make a difference in our physical relationship. I never promised to stop seeing Marco. So, I've carried on.'

I forked some scrambled eggs into my mouth and considered how not promising something that should be obvious might constitute permission.

'Didn't John assume that you would stop when you got married? Didn't Marco assume it was over?'

She shrugged. 'I didn't expect you to understand.'

I imagined her husband as a diminutive, shrivelled little raisin of a man, weak and impotent; a man who swallowed his sadness. A man who dropped his work to look after their daughter, Savannah, while Meredith flew away for weekends of heavy drinking and wild sex.

But what about John's wants and needs? What about Savannah's?

Meredith and Marco's relationship could only be about sex, because if they had a true meeting of minds and hearts, they would have stayed together permanently.

I hoped that her holidays were worth the heartache I was sure they caused. Had Jamie found betrayal a breeze, as Meredith apparently did? Had he given so little consideration to me, Jack, and Oliver while he was out, sowing his oats with Rose? My toast tasted like cardboard.

'Does John really know about you and Marco, and not care?' It seemed unimaginable.

'Yes, I think so.' Meredith combed her hair with her fingers and stared down the garden, lost in thought, then looked back at me. 'I'm lucky. He loves me so much that he just wants me to be happy.'

Tears pricked my eyes. Maybe it was an overreaction caused by tiredness and a roaring hangover but the way she dismissed his feelings, while considering it normal to have two separate relationships, went against everything that I believe in. Imagining Jamie with Rose still makes me angry and jealous and sick to my stomach; I used to turn my feelings of inadequacy and worthlessness inwards whenever he was out late, and torture myself with thoughts of what he might be doing. I hated being irrelevant and discardable. Forgiving Jamie, trying to understand the reasons for his affair, was something I never did. Taking him back had never crossed my mind. So, I knew, instinctively, that Meredith's husband, no matter how old he was, would surely care that she had a lover.

It was none of my business, but I wanted to know more. 'Is John impotent or something?'

A flicker of *mind your fucking business* crossed her face. She lit another cigarette, drew a deep lungful, and blew a plume of smoke into the morning air.

'I'm not completely heartless, Tana – I love John and Savannah. But I was with Marco first and couldn't give him up. He's an ingrained habit. John's fifteen years older than me and no, he isn't impotent – he's actually in very good health – but he's also a laid-back kind of person and pretty open when it comes to sex. I've never hidden Marco from him. We don't talk about it, but he knows I have a holiday fling. Just a bit of fun. John accepts it completely.'

There was nothing to say. I was a guest in Meredith's house, in no position to start preaching my morals, but it made me uncomfortable. She and Marco could have been together properly if they had really wanted to be. Clearly, they didn't. I wasn't going to ask for her life story to try and understand how they had ended up in such a tangled relationship but, in my mind, they were two peas in a selfish pod.

'Does Marco have a family?'

'No. He never married and has no kids.'

That was a relief, although I don't know why I cared. My own kids and their heartbreak were enough to deal with. 'Well, that's one thing, I suppose.'

Even though I wanted and needed to hear more, because Meredith could probably explain what Jamie was thinking while he was seeing Rose, I didn't ask. First, I needed to digest what she had said. The time had to be right.

In silence, she smoked her cigarette and I watched the bees. After a while, I went to phone the boys.

17

Jack and Oliver bubbled with enthusiasm when I called. They took turns relaying a long list of things they had managed to do in the time since I had left them at Jamie's – little more than 24 hours – as well as their plans for the rest of the week, and it put a smile on my face at first.

Yet the more they explained, the more useless I felt and the more I argued with myself: they prefer Jamie / don't be silly / they love him more / no, they don't / he is more fun / but I am reliable … it went on and on.

Jamie is calmer than me for sure, but he doesn't have to deal with the boys every day, so he would be. He is probably more fun too, for the same reason. Still, it seemed that they were rubbing their wonderful plans in my face. Had I suggested tenting out in the garden, they would have rolled their eyes. Had I suggested the cinema, Jack would have turned his nose up and gone with friends. But then I remembered what he had accused me of. Was I making it all about me? Was that my default setting?

In truth, their excitement was because I would never have suggested those things; I am always too low or too stressed, and I also control when and for how long they stay with Jamie. A week is much longer than usual. So, it is natural that they would treat it as a novelty and that he would want to spoil them with things I have neither the time, the money nor the inclination for.

I would never offer a choice of the cinema, the pool, the park, a pizza takeaway, a movie or video games after school. I would never sleep in the tent with them on a Saturday night or toast marshmallows over a bonfire. But Jamie was doing it all. No homework. That would clearly be waiting for me to organise when I got home. No wonder the boys prefer being with him, I thought. I'm boring.

My head was throbbing again, so I took more painkillers and made another coffee. My mind was full of family dynamics – not only my relationship with Jack and Oliver but also their love for Jamie. It led me to consider Meredith's situation from her point of view and I realised that her double life must be the very thing that keeps her happy and full of energy. She described Marco as an ingrained habit, therefore an outlet, an addiction – nothing more. If that works for her, what's it got to do with me?

Confusing as it seemed, her relationship with Marco was interesting; it forced me into some soul searching. Inevitably, I compared our situations. Her husband tolerated her lover – and whilst I could not imagine ever doing that, I wondered if I had overreacted by throwing Jamie out and divorcing him instead of understanding what he did. Or at least trying to understand.

For months afterwards, he had tried to speak to me, maybe to make amends and apologise, before realising that I would not change my mind. That's when he finally stopped sofa surfing at friends' houses and rented a place of his own. It crossed my mind that perhaps it had not been Jamie after all, who destroyed our marriage.

Meredith was cool towards me when I returned to the garden. She was still in her seat, sipping a glass of water. When I sat down, she offered a thin smile.

'I'm sorry I blurted out my opinion,' I said. She lit a cigarette and blew a smoke ring but didn't respond. 'I must be a prude,' I carried on. 'I'm old-fashioned.'

'Marco and I have nothing to do with fashion,' she said.

'Well, I'm sorry if I caused offence – judging something I don't understand.'

Meredith shrugged and sighed deeply. 'Don't worry about it.'

Apologising did not make me feel better. If anything, I was even more conflicted. I figured it must be me, and that maybe everyone is at it.

Maybe affairs are so commonplace that they are unremarkable, beyond judgement. But Meredith did not want to talk about it anymore, so I left her with her friends and went upstairs to pack. I would thank her, call a taxi, and sneak away without having to say goodbye to the others.

While trying to zip my case shut, I heard a quiet knock on the door. Meredith poked her head in and asked if we could talk. Shutting the door behind her, she put a cup of tea and a plate of croissants on the bedside table.

'Are you ok, Tana?' she said. 'It must be overwhelming with everyone here. Especially as you don't speak French.'

'I'm ok, honestly. Thanks for the tea. But I'm going.'

She sat on the edge of the bed and ran her palm over the duvet. 'You don't have to, you know.'

'I do. And I really am sorry about earlier. If it works for you, that's great.' I smiled. 'I'm just jealous because I have no men and you have two.'

Her face glowed when she laughed. 'Well, now you put it like that ...'

'I'll get out of your way, make a move to the hotel and let you spend time with your friends.'

'No, Tana.' She shook her head. 'Please don't, there's no need. It'll be boring there and, now that you know about me and Marco, there'll be no more surprises.'

'But aren't you pissed off with me?'

'I was.' She nodded. 'But I'm not anymore. Although I don't hide anything from people who come here, most aren't so openly judgemental.' She grinned. 'You're feistier than I gave you credit for.'

Pleased with such a description, I grinned. 'Hiding my feelings has never been a strong point. But really, your life is none of my business.'

'It doesn't matter,' she said. 'Honestly. In fact, it's refreshing. Just stay. We'll have a laugh.'

She didn't need to ask again.

After the breakfast washing up was done, the others left, and Meredith and I strolled into town. Nice was bustling and my spirits lifted as we walked and talked, peering into boutiques and curiosity shops in the narrow side streets. It was warm and sunny, and the fresh sea smell was invigorating. Like the day before beside the pool, it felt natural being with her, pointing out a necklace here or a dress there. Time in Nice, spent chatting about everything and nothing, without the worries of school pickup and cooking dinner, finally felt like the space I had come away for.

In the middle of a conversation about clothes, Meredith suddenly grabbed my arm. 'Hang on.'

Like a dog spotting a squirrel, she dashed over to a market stall and picked up what looked like a wide black scarf, then waved it in the air at me while I jostled through the crowd to her.

'What do you think?' she said. 'This will look gorgeous on you.'

I laughed, more out of disbelief than anything else. 'You are joking, aren't you? That won't cover my backside.'

She frowned. 'Don't be silly. You're so self-deprecating. I'm sure you have body dysmorphia.' She held the sliver of fabric in front of me and squinted, head tilted. 'Trust me, this will fit fine. Besides, it's stretchy.'

'What is it anyway?' I asked. 'It doesn't look big enough to be a dress.'

'You're funny.' Meredith laughed and handed the stall owner some Euros. 'Leave it to me to get you sorted for tonight. This is my treat.'

'Tonight? Why, what's happening?' I hoped she would say pizza, a bottle of red and an early night, but figured there was no chance of that if she wanted me to wear the black scarf / dress thing.

'We're going clubbing.' She grinned. 'Oh, come on, don't look like that! It's Saturday night – would be rude not to.'

Sitting at a pavement café, we ordered cappuccinos. My feet were sore from walking so it was nice to take the weight off them, and we sat in comfortable silence, absorbing the street atmosphere.

Glancing into a shop window across the road, I noticed a pair of black strappy sandals that would match the dress and made a snap decision – very unlike my usual 'deliberation and justification' routine when buying new clothes.

Meredith looked amused when I got back. 'Blimey Tana, that was quick.' She smiled at the waitress who had brought our drinks. '*Merci*.'

'Your influence, I'm sure,' I said, stirring sugar into my coffee. I opened the box and showed her the sandals. 'These will go nicely with that dress.'

'They're lovely. You'll look fantastic tonight.'

'We'll see. I'm not convinced it would fit a skeleton. I'll probably look like a sausage bursting out of its skin.'

Meredith laughed loudly and lit a cigarette. 'I promise, you'll look great.' She narrowed her eyes at me. 'We'll get you a man tonight, if you like?'

My stomach flipped. 'What makes you think I want one?'

'I saw you checking out Stefan last night,' she said, one eyebrow raised. 'It would be good for you to have some fun. He'd be up for it.'

I gaped at her, and she laughed again, leaned back in her chair, and said, 'Be honest, when was the last time you had sex?'

'What? That's a bit personal, isn't it?' I took a sip of cappuccino and racked my brains for the answer but came up with nothing. It had to be at least two years.

She watched me squirm, then shook her

head and frowned, making me feel like an alien life-form being observed under a microscope. 'Come on, Tana, let me in,' she said. 'I bet I can help.'

My throat constricted, trying to recall the last time Jamie and I had sex – he was the only person I had slept with. Ever. But I could not remember and wanted to slap Meredith's face because her eyes were glimmering with amusement.

'What are you? A psychiatrist?'

She just smiled and smoked the rest of her cigarette, one arm resting across her stomach and the other propped on the arm of her chair.

'Alright, it was a while ago,' I admitted at last, with a shrug. My stomach was still churning.

'A while?' She leaned in closer. 'Is that a short while or a long while?'

The café was busy and, as she squeezed between our little table and the one next to us, the waitress bumped both. My coffee slopped into the saucer. Grateful for the distraction, I tipped it back into the cup, then took a deep breath and blew it out through rigid lips.

'A long while,' I said, unable to look Meredith in the eye. 'I can't remember exactly. Maybe two years. Maybe three. I've only ever been with Jamie.'

When I looked up, her eyes were wide. 'Three years? Wow. That's a *really* long time.' She looked away, towards the crowds on the other side of the street, apparently lost in thought.

I added more sugar to my coffee and stirred again, waiting for her to say something, wondering why she wasn't. Did she feel sorry for me? I hoped not. Pity would tip me over the edge.

Finally, she turned back to me. There were deep grooves between her eyes. 'What happened?'

I shrugged and blinked, eyes burning. 'You know how it is when you have young kids. I was always exhausted. I felt ugly. We never went out, just the two of us.' Fiddling with my spoon, I confessed. 'I guess I stopped paying him attention. My world revolved around the boys, and Jamie took a back seat. When he had an affair, I kicked him out. Since then, I've not had a flicker of interest from anyone. In fact, I'm beginning to think there's something wrong with me.' Suddenly, my nose felt full of bees. Tears welled, blurring my vision. I slouched in my chair and breathed in short hitches, having failed to sound flippant.

Passing me a serviette, Meredith looked thoughtful. She folded her hands in her lap and sat quietly while my shoulders shook. I dabbed my eyes. We didn't know each other well enough for a comforting hug. After a minute, she patted my hand and gave it a brief squeeze which made me cry harder.

As I sobbed, I told her a condensed

version of my current situation; like Nicky, she listened without comment. Although it was embarrassing to keep crying and unloading, it felt good to speak about Jamie with someone who doesn't know us. By the time I finished, Meredith was smoking another cigarette, deep in thought.

'Do you still love him?' she asked. 'Because that's what it sounds like to me. If you didn't, you'd have moved on by now – I'm sure you would.'

'It's not that easy for someone like me to get a new boyfriend,' I said. 'For you, I'm sure there's a queue of men waiting, but I'm not like you. I'm frumpy.' I smiled. 'And I'm grumpy.' She shook her head and opened her mouth to speak but I held up my hand to stop her. 'I am and I accept that. But in any event, I don't go out much. There aren't many opportunities to meet people, other than at school. And have you seen the playground dads?'

'Yeah.' She laughed and pulled a grimacing face. 'Not much on offer there. It is a dilemma, but nothing is unsolvable.' Chewing the tip of her thumb, she looked at me quizzically. 'You haven't answered my question though. Do you still love him? Because the answer to that, determines everything else.'

'No. Yes. I don't know,' I said. 'I think so. I've loved him from the first time I saw him – cheesy as that sounds. He was my first boyfriend, he's

Jack and Oliver's dad, and he's been my world since I was sixteen. It's hard to switch that off, no matter how much he hurt me.'

'Tell me about it,' she said, clearly thinking of Marco. 'But is there a chance of rekindling your relationship?'

I shook my head. 'Are you kidding? There is literally no chance – we just got divorced. It's the Decree Absolute coming through a couple of weeks ago that sent me over the edge. It's why I'm here. The situation is hopeless. Jamie hates me.' I rolled up one of the empty sugar packets and pressed it against my fingers – anything to avoid looking at Meredith.

'Why does he hate you?' she asked. 'What did you do?'

I shrugged. 'Let's just say I was unreasonable.' The tiny packet felt nice and sharp against my skin, and I squeezed it tighter.

'Most people in your position would be.' Meredith watched the waitress clear the table next to us. 'Splitting up is an ugly business. It can bring out the worst in people.'

'I suppose,' I said. 'But anyway, Jamie probably moved on ages ago, while I was being stubborn and refusing to solve the problems in our relationship.'

She raised her eyebrows. 'What, you stonewalled him?'

I nodded and red shame climbed up my neck. 'Pretty much. I just shut down. He had hurt me so much – I can't begin to explain it.'

'Is that what he wanted then? He wanted to talk things through?'

She was looking intently at me, her lips pursed, and a stabbing pain in my gut told me this was the truth. 'Yeah,' I said quietly. 'I guess it was.'

She thought about this for a minute or two. 'Have you tried cyber-stalking him?' she asked eventually, taking a deep draw on her cigarette, and blowing the smoke upwards. 'You know, to see whether he's got a girlfriend?'

'Cyber what? Oh, do you mean on the internet? I doubt I'd find much, it's not like he's famous or anything.'

Meredith laughed again. 'No need to look so shocked but yeah, I mean looking him up on Facebook or MySpace, or Twitter. Loads of people have social media accounts these days and, if Jamie does, we can find him. See what he's been up to.'

'It's never crossed my mind. Do people really do that?'

'Yes, of course they do! Where have you been living, in a cave?' She stubbed out her cigarette and rubbed her hands together as if formulating a plan. 'Honestly, Tana, if you're not on social media, you're unusual. People mostly use it to show off how great they look, or how much they spoil their kids, or where they are on holiday. But others use it to be nosy.'

'Sounds weird. Our computer doesn't get used much – the boys play that Club Penguin game and I check my emails, but that's about it.'

'Well then, it's time you were dragged into the 21st century. You're only a decade late!' Her eyes gleamed. 'Tell you what, I've got a Facebook account. Let's look Jamie up when we get back to the house.'

Two hours later, Meredith logged on. It was fascinating. She had hundreds of friends, and loads of photos, mainly shots of her daughter, Savannah. But there were also many of Meredith and John, as well as the three of them together – seemingly a perfect family. Knowing the truth behind the pictures saddened me. Meredith would never admit that her life is a lie, she claims they are happy, but I know what it is like to live with an unfaithful partner. It hit me like a brick that my circumstances were preferable.

Feeling a little bit sick, I watched over Meredith's shoulder as she typed "Jamie Malone" into the search bar. Numerous matches came up and we scrolled through the list until I saw him. It was a nice picture; he looked tanned and healthy, clearly a holiday shot, and I wondered where he was, who took the photo, and whether he still smiles that way for her.

'That's him.' I pointed to his profile picture.

Meredith swivelled her head to look at me. 'You ok? You sound strangled.'

'I'm fine,' I said. 'It just feels a bit wrong to be doing this. Intrusive.'

She grinned. 'You'll get over it.' Clicking on Jamie's account, she studied the picture. 'He's attractive. I can't believe I've never noticed him at school before.'

Something in her voice sounded like surprise and I assumed she meant I had done well for myself, that I'd been punching above my weight. Maybe it is insecurity, but I had always felt that he was too good looking for me, that we didn't match in that way, and maybe deep down I had always expected to lose him to someone else. I murmured something non-committal in response, and she turned again to look at me.

'Oh, I'm sorry – that was out of order. I didn't think.'

'Don't worry,' I said through gritted teeth. 'I'm used to it.'

'Really?' she said.

'Yep. All you need to do now, is say how much my handsome sons look like Jamie.'

Meredith squinted and wrinkled her nose up. 'Do people say that?' she asked. 'Well, I haven't seen your older son for ages, but Oliver's the dead spit of you. And he's gorgeous. I've said it before, Tana, you have a very warped image of yourself.' She turned back to the screen, and I wiped my brimming tears.

Jamie's account had no security, so we looked at everything. Meredith was right, the sense of spying soon wore off. His marital status was single, which surprised me; I had always assumed that Rose was the first in a line, or that by now Jamie would have found himself a new partner, but we looked at every photo and comment and found no evidence of a girlfriend. There were comments from women, and photos of him and his friends with women I didn't recognise, but nothing that screamed of a relationship.

He had posted a selfie just a few hours before, with Jack and Oliver on either side of him. They were on a park bench, all leaning into the frame, pulling goofy faces. The caption said, 'Hanging out with my boys.'

'That's sweet,' Meredith said.

'Yeah.' I could barely speak.

Jamie looked proud and the boys looked happy, but the comments hurt. His friends had written things like, 'Quality time at last!' and 'Enjoy every moment!' One joker had reminded him that kidnap is illegal.

Was I that bad at letting him see them? He usually only has them for a few days per fortnight because that's what I offered. That's what he agreed to. However, looking at his online world it seemed that he wanted more, and I realised that I hadn't given him any choice. Had he agreed to everything I specified when we split up because he felt guilty and hadn't wanted to make things worse?

'So, what do you think?' Meredith asked, after we had looked at all of Jamie's photos and statuses for the past year or so. 'Have you found out anything important?'

'Not about whether he's in a relationship,' I said, 'but I'm starting to realise a few other things.'

18

Getting into the sausage-skin dress was memorable. I had pulled it down over my head but, despite being super stretchy, it twisted and rolled, trapping my arms as I tried to wiggle into it. When Meredith pushed the door open, I was a sweating, cursing mess with my whole body on show.

'Tana, I –' she was saying, then gasped and started giggling. 'Oh, my goodness, let me help you!'

Grasping the dress, she unrolled it down me, over my arms and shoulders, wriggled it straight and finally yanked it over my backside. All the while, I stood there like a toddler. By the time she turned me towards the mirror, we were both laughing.

'Et voila!' she said.

My reflection stopped me laughing. How had Meredith known? The dress was little more than a tube of fabric with gathers which allowed for stretch, but it clung in all the right places. The cap sleeves covered my upper arms and flattered my shoulders, my tummy was flat, my hips were curvy, and the sweetheart neckline showcased my cleavage. Meredith had lent me a push-up bra and the results were spectacular, even if I did say so myself.

I wondered why I hid under jeans and baggy sweatshirts when it was possible to look like this. My impulse-buy sandals matched perfectly too. I couldn't remember ever feeling so confident and pretty. I couldn't believe it was me in the mirror.

Meredith looked me over, admiring her handiwork. 'You scrub up alright.' She smiled, watching me twirl and preen. 'So, do you still miss Jamie, or are you just gutted that he cheated?'

I carried on admiring my reflection, too absorbed in my transformation to give much consideration to her question. 'What do you mean?'

'Well, I mean there's a massive difference between being genuinely stuck on someone because you love them and fixating on them out of anger and bitterness.' She picked up the hairbrush I'd left on the bed and began untangling the ends of her hair. 'Be honest, would you take him back?'

I stopped twirling and stared at my reflection. The woman I saw was nice looking, shapely, and she looked great in her new dress. Her hair was healthy and shiny, with no premature greys. She had no wrinkles. Her smile was infectious. I liked her; she deserved happiness. This woman showed no signs of the sadness and self-doubt that I lug around like a suitcase full of rocks, and I realised that those things must therefore only exist in my head. Only a few weeks away from thirty, the woman in the mirror had a future that could be whatever she wanted – but she had to release Jamie, to move forward.

'I don't know if I'd take him back,' I said. 'But you're right, there is a massive difference between love and fixation.' The woman in the mirror suddenly looked sad and pensive, so I looked away in case she started crying.

Turning to Meredith, I said, 'For a long time, I've been angry with Jamie. So, so angry. I've also been confused about why he had an affair.' I sat on the bed and buckled my sandals, trying to figure out how to explain. 'We went through so much together, and he is the boys' father. We'll always have that connection. It's difficult … I've always wished we could get back together, but if he suggested it, I don't know if I would. Does that make sense?'

Meredith nodded. 'It does. You wish you'd never split up in the first place because you'd still be with him. But you'd only get back together if it could be as it was at the start. And that's not possible.'

'That's it, in a nutshell,' I said. 'It could never happen, but even in theory I can't risk being hurt again. All relationships carry that risk, of course, but I can't bear the thought of being alone for

211

the rest of my life either. It's a dilemma.' I opened my mascara and started applying it. 'There's no chance of us getting back together anyway. Too much time has passed. He's probably had loads of girlfriends, and I couldn't deal with that.'

'It didn't look that way on Facebook.'

'I know – but Jamie might just keep that stuff secret to protect Jack and Oliver. Let's face it, he cheated on me and never contested anything in the divorce proceedings. He just agreed with everything I asked for and let it go through as quickly as possible. That doesn't sound like someone who wants to stay together, does it?'

Meredith frowned as she thought about it. Then she shrugged. 'I suppose not. The way you tell it, it does sound very cut and dried. Still, tonight you look amazing, so it's his loss.' She held her hand out to me. 'Come on, let's go down to the garden for a drink.'

It was still warm, and we drank more gin and tonics while waiting for her friends. A nightclub loomed but, secretly, I wished we could stay there for the rest of the night, just chatting. The garden darkened. The solar lights flicked on.

'Tell me,' I said, 'was it was possible for Jamie to love me and the boys, and still sleep with someone else?' If anyone could answer that question, Meredith could. I have always been sure that Jamie didn't love Rose and that their affair was just easy sex. But for me, that's what makes it worse, not better. It's hard for me to get my head around because in my world, intimacy is physical, emotional, and mental. I can't separate sex from love, but Meredith can and, presumably, so can Jamie. One possible answer was that he didn't love me anymore, but I still needed her insight to know why. I didn't think I had done anything wrong.

Without missing a beat, she said, 'It was totally possible to love you and sleep with someone else. Totally.' She sipped her drink and crunched a little ice chip before shooting an arrow straight through me. 'To be honest, I bet he didn't think about it too much. I reckon it was simple – he was needy, and she was there, ready to provide.'

'What do you mean by needy?' I asked. 'What did she provide that I didn't?'

Meredith looked at me as if I had just fallen from the sky. 'Sex, obviously. It's pretty much all that men think about.'

'But … it wasn't as if we weren't having any at all. It just wasn't very often. I was tired from looking after the boys and working.'

Meredith shook her head. 'You said it yourself; you were stressed out and down in the dumps – you hadn't been having much.' She broke off and took another sip, holding my gaze. 'Look, I don't know Jamie at all so might be wrong, but from what I know of men generally, they need food, comfort and regular servicing.'

'This is my ex-husband we're discussing – not a car engine.'

She laughed. 'I know, but they have their similarities.'

I sighed. My gin was strong and burned my throat. 'Sounds like you've got it sussed.' I didn't care how sarcastic I sounded. She made me feel like an innocent.

'I haven't, believe me. But in my experience, keep them satisfied in bed and they're happier in general. I think men need sex to regulate their temper.'

Without having slept with anyone else, I had to take her word for it, but Jamie had always seemed more cheerful after we'd slept together so it sounded plausible.

'Maybe you're right. I wasn't thinking much about his needs at the time though; I was just trying to get through each day, juggling two little boys, a house, and a job.'

'Hey, you don't have to justify it to me. I'm not saying anything bad about you, Tana. You asked for my opinion, and I've given it.' She lit a cigarette. 'It's hard, it's all hard ... motherhood, relationships ... you don't learn any of this important stuff at school, do you?'

I shook my head and bit my lip. I wanted to explain what it had been like for me, because she had no idea. Beautiful Meredith, with her family, her friends, her rich husband, her French lover, and only one child to deal with – she could never begin to understand my life. She could not imagine working in the evening after a disturbed night's sleep and a full day at home. Week after week, month after month, year after year. It was shattering. Looking after Jamie and his sexual requirements had not been my top priority, and she was not going to make me feel guilty.

'It was more complicated than that,' I said. 'There was so much going on – I was exhausted, and sex was the last thing I felt like doing. After Oliver was born, I felt fat and ugly and didn't want Jamie to see me naked. My body repulsed me, and I figured it would repulse him too. I just wanted to sleep. Oliver was going through this phase where he kept waking up all night and …' I trailed off, lost in the memories.

'I understand that Tana, I really do. But maybe Jamie didn't. He was at work all day and didn't have to contend with the relentlessness of small children. Like I said, men need plenty of sex and to know that they're loved, so maybe he felt rejected and frustrated. He might have felt jealous of the boys too.'

'But I didn't reject him.'

'Hey, I'm just playing devil's advocate. I'm saying it's *possible* that that's how Jamie felt. If his life lacked sex and comfort, he might have just taken them both where he could find them.'

She took a deep drag on her cigarette, making the orange tip glow brightly, then exhaled into the dark blue above her head.

'So, you're saying it's all my fault.'

'Tana. Listen to me. I'm not saying anything of the kind.' She ground out her cigarette and ran her fingers through her long hair. 'I just know what I know. I'm willing to bet that he thought it would be a quick, one-off shag – no strings attached and no consequences – but it got out of hand. I'm not justifying what he did, obviously, but I doubt his thoughts or feelings were involved. I bet it was purely physical.' She held up one finger to stop me interjecting. 'What I mean is, I think he thought with his dick and regretted it later. I don't believe he set out to hurt you and destroy your family.'

My stomach churned. Putting my glass down, I said, 'That's pretty much what he said happened. He told me it started at the office Christmas party.'

'There you go.' She sat back and crossed her legs, studying me. 'What did you say?'

'I told him he was a cliché.'

She laughed. 'Yeah, sounds like it.'

I felt bruised. She had certainly provided the insight I'd asked for. Everyone I have talked to about Jamie has gone down the, 'He's an arse, a cheater, you're better off without him,' road. Not Meredith.

'But that's exactly what I don't understand,' I said, hugging my arms across my chest. '*How* can you do all those things with someone else, without it causing pain and destruction? It makes no sense.'

I knew that this was not only about Jamie but also a direct blow at Meredith and Marco. But how could I mention one without insinuating the other?

She leaned towards me and squeezed my trembling hand, having obviously learned the signs of my impending tears. 'There's something you have to understand,' she said. 'I might be wrong, but from everything you've said, I doubt it. Fact 1: Jamie had an affair. It was probably the first time, and it was probably something random that lasted longer than it should have. Fact 2: When you found out about it you went ballistic and kicked him out of the house – no discussion, no trying. Fact 3: Just because *you* wouldn't have done what he did, doesn't mean that it's impossible to comprehend. Affairs happen.'

That was it, summarised. I'd been going in circles trying to understand Jamie's behaviour, but the only yardstick I had to measure it by was my own strict morality. With such limited parameters, his actions would never fit with my expectations. It struck me that my parents probably felt the same way when we told them I was pregnant. But Meredith understood Jamie's actions perfectly. To her, they were simple. I supposed that if I ever wanted to deal with the situation, I'd have to consider it from her point of view. Or better yet, from Jamie's.

We sat in silence, sipping our drinks. I was glad I'd asked her, but it was quite a lot to take in. The sky grew even darker, and moths whirled around the garden lights.

'It seems strange, asking someone as unconventional as you for relationship advice,' I said after a while, 'but what you've said does make sense.'

Meredith's face was hard to see clearly in the shadows, but her head dropped forwards. 'Well, just because I'm unconventional, doesn't mean I can't see what's going on,' she said quietly. 'In my humble opinion, the reason so many relationships fail is because people can't see the bigger picture. Marriage is hard work, especially when kids are involved.'

'It sure is,' I agreed.

She pulled her hair back and wrapped it into a loose ponytail. 'You see it all the time – tired women, and men feeling rejected in favour of the children. What happened between you and Jamie is happening in millions of homes. The difference between things working and failing, as far as I see it, is compromise and empathy.'

'Sorry, but I disagree,' I replied, my palms feeling prickly. 'Jamie's affair was entirely his fault. Why should I have empathised with him? What he did was rotten – it was unfair and selfish. Are you saying I should have accepted responsibility for what he did?'

'No, I'm not saying that at all,' Meredith said

calmly, 'but I think that your response was very knee-jerk. You didn't factor in the consequences or consider why he did it. Had you worked together, you might have found that his affair breathed new life into your marriage.'

'What? Are you serious?' I almost shouted it. 'How could I have lived with him after hearing what he'd been up to?'

'Well, you obviously couldn't, which is why you let your emotions guide you, and divorced him. But it seems to me that you've never forgiven yourself for that decision, which means it might not have been the right one.'

A punch in the stomach would not have winded me as much.

'Bloody hell,' I said, 'you should be an agony aunt. Or a counsellor. You're good at this.'

As cross as I was, I could see the sense in what she was saying. I drained the last of my drink, feeling the alcohol numbing me, soothing my mind.

'But what I don't get is why you think it's my fault.'

'Tana,' she cried, 'I don't think it's your fault! When have I said that?'

I shrugged. She hadn't said it explicitly, but I felt it there, lurking.

She finished her drink and said, 'I'm going to try to make this clear. Listen closely. I understand why you did what you did, but I can also understand what Jamie did. I'm not saying it's anybody's fault – that is your interpretation of what I'm saying. You need to forget about fault because you're stuck on it but, once again, that's your guilt talking. Lose the guilt and step back a bit; try looking at your situation objectively. That's what I'm doing as I'm not involved. You might see everything in a new light.'

God, she even sounded like Jamie, but I thought she was a hypocrite. How could she talk about empathy and compromise, when she was leading her husband a merry dance? Although she wasn't preaching about honesty in a relationship, it seemed to me that she thought she had all the answers, when her own marriage is a sham.

'What about you then?' I asked finally, still feeling defensive. 'Where's all the understanding and compromise in your relationship? You're leading a double life in effect, so you don't exactly practice what you preach.'

It came out with more venom than I'd intended but I didn't apologise. Meredith doesn't temper her opinions, so I decided not to either. She didn't react, just inspected her nails.

'I know all of that; do you think I don't?' She sighed. 'But seeing Marco actually helps my marriage.' She raised her hand again, to stop me interrupting. 'Marco is a sideline. Coming here allows me to be the person I was when I was young. When I'm here with my friends, real life takes a backseat. When I go home, I'm all refreshed and ready to face whatever family life can throw at me.'

I couldn't believe the utter bullshit I was hearing. I mean, we'd all like to go back to being young and carefree several times a year, wouldn't we? But that's not reality.

'What about Marco?' I asked. 'Aren't you just using him? Does he like being a sideline?'

She nodded. 'He doesn't mind at all – it's the same for him. We know exactly what we are to one another, so neither of us feels used or jealous. It's just a bit of no-strings fun.'

To me, this sounded cripplingly immature, but I didn't want to argue. Our differences had been clear for ages, and I wasn't sure whether she made me angry, jealous, or indignant – probably all three – but I was learning how conventional I am.

'Lucky you,' I said. 'I'd love for my life to be put on the back burner every couple of months.'

'It's what you're doing now, isn't it?'

'No. Nothing like it.'

'You're wrong. It's exactly the same.'

'No, it's not,' I retorted, suddenly feeling ridiculous in my new outfit. 'I came away to try and get my head together, to sort out my feelings and get my life back on track. It's a one-off.'

Meredith shook her head and spoke slowly. 'You can deny it all you like, but coming here is an escape from reality, from ordinary, everyday life.' She sounded a bit bored. 'You came to get away from your problems in the hope that they'd be lessened by your absence. That's all I'm saying and that's all I'm doing too – I just do it more regularly.'

I sat back, aware of my clenched fists and heavy breathing. My heart was pounding. Half of me wanted to slap her while the other was impressed by her honesty. Taking deep breaths and releasing them slowly, I forced my fingers to uncurl. Meredith, of course, looked perfectly relaxed, utterly composed. In the half light, I saw a faint smile dance across her mouth.

'I know you're going to find this inconceivable,' she said, 'but I love them all. It's unusual and sounds impossible, but I really do. I always loved Marco and could never give him up because he's a connection to my youth, but what I have at home is security and motherhood. I don't think about home when I'm here, and vice versa.'

How could she not think about home – her daughter? I had thought loads about Jack and Oliver. She sounded like a rambling mad woman.

'You're right,' I said. 'I can't understand that at all. You seem to have the perfect life at home; you have a caring husband and a lovely child who never causes you any trouble, yet you're risking it all for a fantasy – a relationship which might have been but never was. You and Marco could have been together properly if you'd really wanted it.'

'I know,' Meredith conceded. She tipped the leftover ice from her glass into her mouth and crunched it. 'But it's been like this for so long now that I can't live my life any other way. John is wonderful and saved me from myself when I was younger; he earns great money and looks after us well. But he's a lot older than me. Marco was always my love. I think I'm just not cut out for monogamy.'

A quick snort escaped my nose, and I shook my head. 'You know,' I said, 'I spend my whole life worrying. I worry that I am a crap mother, I worry about whether I did the right thing in chucking Jamie out and divorcing him, I tear my hair out over the boys' behaviour and I chastise myself, assuming they're naughty because of something I did wrong. Every time I consider who I am, the choices I made when I was young and what I'm doing with my life now, I drown in self-doubt and self-recrimination. I lack confidence and my inner voice relentlessly tells me I'm wrong, bad, lacking – just not good enough. And I don't expect you to understand why I came here, but it was to try and organise – even exorcise – these thoughts. To be honest, your reasons feel less ... well ... urgent. Sorry if that sounds judgemental.'

Meredith nodded and I noticed her eyes looked shiny. 'It does, but I promise you, I know where you're coming from.'

'How could you know?' I looked at the sky,

feeling my own tears welling. As the darkness deepened, a rich seam of navy blue lined the treetops, and a bat circled above us.

'Why do you think I couldn't?' she asked.

'Because you're the total opposite of me. You seem to breeze through life with everything going your way, living in a situation I could never have imagined before today. But, regardless of your relationship with John, I just don't get how you could do it to Savannah.'

'Do what to her, precisely?' Meredith's tone was a knife.

I'd said too much. She did not fit my image of a good mother, but it's never a good idea to criticize anyone's parenting skills. Suddenly, my sheltered upbringing felt like a burden – it was clear I lacked life experience. My parents had saddled me with rigid ideas about behaviour and morals, but Meredith's lifestyle was teaching me to break those moulds. I could see that just because someone might not conduct themselves as I would, that doesn't make them wrong. More importantly, it doesn't make me right.

'Sorry, I didn't mean it like that,' I said, back-pedalling. 'I just ... I don't know, she's brilliantly looked after and everything ... she must just wonder why you're away so much. And you must miss her.'

Meredith stared at me through letterbox eyes. 'Savannah's a star. She's a great kid and I love her. The thing is, she's never known anything different, and we have an au pair who she adores and who looks after her well. Plus, I'm only ever away for a matter of days.' She lit another cigarette, and a shower of tiny sparks flew from the flint in her lighter. 'Many parents see their kids less than I see Savannah, without leaving the country,' she said. 'Parents who work long hours, for example.'

I nodded, unsure of whether to agree.

'The thing is, Tana, from what I see there are a load of parents who are in the room with their kids, but barely give them the time of day. They're talking on the phone or watching TV or just plain tired.' She stared at me. 'When I am with Savannah, we do stuff together. We have fun, play games, chat, read, bake, paint. I don't think I can be judged a bad parent if that's what you're saying.'

'Oh God, no – that's not what I'm saying at all. You're right. There are all sorts out there.'

I was desperate to change the subject but only one person I wanted to change it back to. There was one more thing I needed to ask. We sat for an uncomfortable minute or two, and I wondered if she was angry. Eventually, I took the plunge.

'Do you think Jamie just agreed to everything during our divorce because he didn't care and wanted to get out quickly? Or do you think it was because he felt guilty?' I asked. 'I have questioned it a million times and still don't know.'

Meredith twisted in her seat and tucked her feet up. She wiped the glowing tip of her cigarette into the ashtray, pulled a packet of Rizla papers from her handbag and crumbled the remains of her half-smoked cigarette into one. Then she opened a small plastic pouch and sprinkled something from it on top of the tobacco. With a lick and an expert flick, she rolled it up and put it in her mouth before lighting it and drawing deeply. A sweet pungent smell wafted over on the evening air.

Just as I was wondering whether she'd heard me, she replied. 'I reckon he felt guilty.'

'Do you really?'

'Yeah.' She paused, thinking it through, blowing the smoke out of her nose. 'I reckon he felt terrible, so agrccd to everything to minimise hassle. His way of making amends. He was probably hoping things could be amicable between you. Very few people are incapable of caring, Tana. I don't think Jamie's a psychopath.' She leaned forward and held her joint towards me. 'Do you want some?'

'Is it weed?'

She laughed. 'Yes. Don't tell me you've never smoked before.'

The incredulity in Meredith's tone suggested I was blinkered and small-minded. It said how much I have missed. There and then I decided that my holiday would be the opposite of what I planned. It would be a time to experience new things, loosen up, gain a wider appreciation of life, and make up for lost time.

'Well, no – I haven't.'

'Do you want to try it?' Meredith asked. 'You don't have to, but it'll be fine, I promise.'

The whole scenario felt naughty. But it was a thrill to be bad. Taking the joint tentatively, I marvelled at the unfamiliar feel of its heat between my fingers, and let the smell evoke memories of Jamie and our evenings on the rocks in Newquay. My heart hammered as I put it to my lips and copied how Meredith smokes, sucking hard and inhaling deep.

A stinking, burning juggernaut rushed down into my lungs, setting my throat on fire as it invaded every cell, exploded in my chest and made me cough uncontrollably. My eyes streamed and I couldn't catch my breath, much to Meredith's amusement.

'Have you never even smoked cigarettes?'

'No,' I rasped, through a spasm of coughing. 'Not once.'

'Here, take a sip.' She could hardly speak for giggling but handed me my glass.

I drank the melting ice. The coughing subsided but my chest ached, and my throat smouldered. I wiped my eyes and saw black streaks of mascara on my fingers.

'Sorry,' she said, stifling a giggle. 'I should have warned you – it's quite strong.'

'No kidding. It almost blew my head off.'

But as soon as I stopped coughing, I wanted more. At least I knew what to expect. The second time was better; I inhaled less and barely coughed at all, and the way it clouded my mind was worth the disgusting taste. I offered it back to Meredith, who shook her head, so I took a few more hits and inhaled deeply, holding each one for a few seconds. Time slowed, just a bit.

Nodding, I said, 'It's good stuff,' as if I knew. She laughed.

My face felt fixed in grin mode, but my stomach wasn't so happy. It twisted and stabbed but I ignored it and let the world slow. A numbing lethargy overcame me – a delay between thought and action. My arms felt heavy and my hand holding the joint looked alien. Looking at Meredith, who was still laughing, the whole situation seemed so bizarre. We were absurd; two unlikely friends sharing stories and new experiences under the late summer sky.

The self-consciousness which blights my existence took a backseat. I got steadily stoned, and Meredith and I laughed as if we would never stop. Everything was great, everything was funny, and everything was calm. Everything in England was distant: my job, my divorce, my melancholy – even the boys. I just wanted to savour the moment, enjoy the freedom. An alternative me sat by the pool, the one in the dress; the one who might have been. She was like

Meredith.

I offered the joint again, but she waved my hand away. 'Finish it. I'll roll another.'

There was no need to say it twice. I smoked the rest and let the mellow feeling wash over me. The atmosphere was good. Life felt fine. I heard crickets and the last of the birdsong. Breathing deeply and slowly, a heightened sense of being alive coincided with complete relaxation; my mind was cocooned in a soft, protective wrapper. Even my internal commentator stopped asking who I am, where I'm going, who likes me, what people think of me, what they think of the boys.

After a while it whispered: 'Were we talking about Jamie?'

But I couldn't remember.

19

I would have been happy to chill by the pool and then go to bed, but Stefan and Marco arrived, and we went out. I guess the girls had other plans.

Meredith said the club was her favourite, and I could see why. It was a huge, crowded, air-conditioned neon palace, with lasers, strobes, dry ice, and foam. They played all the summer bangers loud enough to split eardrums, with bass heavy enough to reverberate through your chest.

The weed cushioned me from most of the mayhem though, and I was happy to sit and watch the sweaty, gyrating clubbers jostling for space, punching their fists up into the air with the beat. Everyone was smiling, laughing, singing, and small groups danced together, acting out the lyrics. When the DJ whipped them into a frenzy, the floor bounced beneath my feet.

Meredith and Marco missed it all though; they sat intertwined on a couch and stared into each other's eyes, canoodling, whispering, kissing. I may not have approved of the relationship, but their chemistry was undeniable.

Stefan sat beside me and handed me a cocktail. *'Soixante quinze,'* he said, *'avec Champagne.'*

'Merci,' I said, taking a sip. It was delicious – tangy and lemony.

He looked great in black jeans and a slim-fitting T shirt, with his silver chain standing out bright against his tanned skin. His spicy, fresh scent awoke my senses, and I wanted him, though the thought of it was scary. I had only ever been attracted to Jamie.

Stefan nudged me, pointed to Meredith and Marco, and rolled his eyes. I laughed and then, in a very smooth and probably practised move, he gently turned my face and planted a soft kiss on my mouth. It was so light, so unexpected.

I should have been angry, but instead the tenderness conveyed by his warm, full mouth almost provoked tears. After freezing for a second, all the hurt, pain, and passion buried deep inside me exploded. Heat flooded my body, and I wrapped my arms around him. The whole world could have stopped right then, and I wouldn't have cared. I'd have died happy. All I knew was his mouth and hands, his slender fingers roaming my shoulders and neck, exploring under my hair, pulling gently, suggesting an urgency which throbbed through me too.

When Jamie rejected me for a younger woman, I was destroyed. Turning his infidelity upon myself because I wasn't "enough", whatever that means, I hid myself away under shapeless clothes and munched family-sized bags of crisps. I guzzled bottles of red wine after the boys went to bed. I watched rubbish TV, to numb the hurt. These things are fine occasionally but every night is dangerous. My bully inner voice said I was ugly, plain, invisible, unlovable, and I believed it when it said I was destined to be alone. That voice still tells me these things all the time but now, after Stefan, I'm shutting it down next time it pipes up. Because when I was kissing him, I knew the voice was wrong.

Stefan was attracted to me, and I felt the sexiest I had in years, the most daring, the most powerful. Meredith had helped me sparkle again, and Stefan was proof of it. When he pulled me to my feet, indicating the door, I didn't hesitate for a second. Glancing over at Meredith, I caught her eye, and she winked and smiled in a way that made me wonder for a moment whether she'd engineered the whole thing. But I didn't care. Paranoia was not going to ruin the moment.

We pushed our way through the dancers to the exit, our hands hot and sweaty, into a crowded street, where the smell of frying onions from the hot dog vendor across the road hung heavy in the air. The night was lit by neon signs. Disorientated by the booze and weed, the world came at me in a series of snapshots. With no idea where we were, or how to get back to Meredith's, all I cared about was Stefan and what I wanted him to do to me. I was in that single-minded state of intoxication where surroundings blur and you imagine that nobody else can see or hear you, and I had to have him. It didn't matter where or how.

Stumbling along the road in my strappy, heeled sandals, I pulled him by the hand and hunted for a private place – a doorway, a hedge, anywhere. No strings, no shame, no comeback. Then I spotted an alleyway between two buildings and dashed across the road, straight into it, neither knowing nor caring what Stefan thought.

He laughed as I kicked aside bottles and rubbish, packets, and wrappers, even a half-eaten burger, searching for the right spot. The alley widened, and we found ourselves in a small yard area behind the shops, lit only by moonlight, where industrial bins overflowed with bulging rubbish bags. Next to one bin was a stack of empty cardboard beer boxes.

Perfect.

Forgetting about everyone and everything, I kissed Stefan again, backing onto the boxes and pulling him closer, fumbling with his belt and the top button of his jeans. A flash of puzzlement crossed his face, but I was insistent, and he didn't argue. Grinning, he yanked my dress up. I didn't care about how I looked or what he thought of me; all I cared about was the moment. This was a one-off conscious decision, forget the consequences, and I forced away all the default thoughts about covering up, or shame.

Can you miss what you've never had before? I don't know, but it felt like my whole life I'd been missing out on down and dirty, up-an-alley sex with a stranger. Well, he wasn't a complete stranger, I told myself. We had met once.

The boxes cushioned my back from the rough brick wall as we stood and kissed, and I remember pushing Stefan away, just a bit, to look and make sure. He stood before me, a shadowy outline with his jeans around his ankles. Most definitely what I wanted. Empowered by his obvious enthusiasm, I linked my fingers together around the back of his neck, pulled his face to mine and kissed him deeply, trying to ignore the boxes' pointy corners which jabbed my backside.

Stefan wrapped one arm around my waist and lightly dusted my breast with the other, his thumb circling my nipple. The thin fabric of my dress allowed for maximum sensation with minimum friction. It was almost too much; I held his face hard against mine while we kissed and he explored my body: clutching, squeezing, and probing.

'I'll leave them here,' I murmured, tugging off my knickers and throwing them.

Stefan built up a rolling rhythm I could scarcely comprehend, it had been so long.

There was no time for control, thought, embarrassment. Gasping for breath, I wrapped my arms around his neck and my legs around his hips, clinging tight until the dam broke and we collapsed onto the broken boxes in the dirty alleyway, laughing while the flood waves subsided.

20

Stretching like a starfish in bed the next morning, I relived every delicious second of my encounter with Stefan. The sheets felt smoother, the pillows plumper, and every inch of my body was diffused with warmth.

Meredith knocked. 'Tana? You awake?' She came in wearing a yellow sundress, fluffy slippers, and a mischievous smile. 'Come on then,' she said, putting a steaming mug of tea on the bedside table. 'Tell me everything!'

'What do you mean? Nothing happened.'

'Yeah, right,' she laughed. 'As if I'd believe that.' I could barely hold my face still as she folded herself into the little armchair by the window and pressed her palms together, mouth twitching. 'Spill the beans.'

It was impossible to hold back. I relaxed against the pillows and told her as much as I could bear to admit, smiles escaping from behind my hand, my cheeks getting hotter as her eyes got wider.

'And that's all I'm saying.'

For several moments she stared like a small child given a longed-for present, then burst out laughing. 'Oh. My. God!' she cried, clapping her hands. 'That is amazing!'

It was like being ten again, when my best friend told me how she had kissed a boy in our class – but back then I had been the one relishing all the gory details.

'I never imagined you'd actually have sex with him.'

'I can't believe I did,' I said. 'It was reckless. Incredible but reckless.'

'Don't worry,' she said. 'Stefan's prepared. I'm sure he used a condom.'

A pang flashed through my chest. For a moment it hurt to be a number. Then I shrugged. The experience was a one-off. Mutually satisfying, but ultimately self-gratifying. Nothing more. We had both got what we needed and had fun in the process.

'I think he did,' I said, remembering a moment of fumbling and hesitation. 'Does he shag around then?'

Meredith looked away; her mouth wrinkled in thought. Let's just say he's popular. But I'm shocked that you went for it too.'

'Not as shocked as I am.' I ran my fingers through my hair, remembering how Stefan had tugged handfuls the night before. 'But I'm glad I did.'

We spent the rest of the morning doing spa-day things: manicures, pedicures, facials, and deep conditioning our hair. Watching Meredith squish her toes into a spongy separator and paint her nails with *Coral Dream* varnish, I understood her love for Nice; it's another world. Even after just two days I felt like a different person. An awake person. It seemed like eons since I had stacked shelves and rotated fresh food in the supermarket fridges, and I realised how much I hate my job. Originally, working had been intended as a short-term measure when our budget was tight but, somehow, I had stayed.

Meredith waved her hand in front of my face. 'Wakey wakey.'

'Sorry?' I said, shaking my thoughts away. 'What did you say?'

'I said you're gawping like a dead fish.'

I grinned. 'Just musing. Being here with no distractions is making things clearer.

'I disagree. You were very distracted last night.'

'Stefan was a welcome one,' I said, stretching my arms and marvelling that my muscles were loose.

'So it seems.' She blew on the wet nail varnish and laughed. 'Who knew?'

'I know, right? I've never done anything like that before.'

'No regrets?' Meredith capped the bottle and handed it to me, eyebrows raised.

Shaking my head, I said, 'No.'

Last night I'd been attractive. Stefan had wanted me, and his attention made the club disappear, foam and all. It had been incredible.

'No regrets at all.'

She smiled and said she was glad.

Picturing myself over the last few years, as stuck in a metaphorical boat being swept along a river, following its meanders, striking its obstacles, and tumbling over its waterfalls, I regretted how little I have taken charge of my life. But I also realised that with Stefan I'd been steering. It was an empowering analogy. Being with Stefan reminded me that there is more to life than monotonous routine, and I promised to remember that in the future, when things at home get fractious.

Speaking of which, just a few nights before I came away, the boys were play-wrestling on the front room floor. I knew Oliver would get hurt because he always does – Jack is bigger and stronger, so their 'fun' often ends in tears. They ignored my warnings to be careful; they ignored me shouting stop; they ignored my threat of sanctions and, inevitably, Jack's elbow caught Oliver's lip, which split.

Although I knew it was accidental, I lost my temper and slapped Jack. Then I stamped upstairs, slammed my bedroom door, and sobbed on my bed for an hour. This is what I'm talking about – if that's not a hostile environment with ineffective, childish parenting, I don't know what is. But I can't stop losing control.

Of course, I didn't mention any of that to

Meredith. Over brunch though, I asked her if life had turned out as she'd envisioned – if she was the parent she'd hoped to be.

'Is this about me, or you?'

I dipped a toast soldier into my boiled egg and runny yolk spilled down the side. 'Both, I guess,' I said, scooping the yellow goo with my finger and licking it off. 'But my life is literally nothing like I thought it would be. I never imagined having kids for a start.'

'Oh, I always wanted children,' she said. 'I'd have liked three but after Savannah I never fell pregnant again.' She shrugged. 'Probably most people end up somewhere unexpected.'

Opening her bacon sandwich, she squirted in ketchup, and squashed the top back on. 'I think that when you're young you feel invincible. Your ideas seem straightforward; you don't anticipate complications. But life throws curve balls.'

'It's not fair though, is it? Some people have a lot more shit to deal with than others.'

Meredith took a bite of her sandwich and chewed, thinking. 'Why should it be fair? Equality is impossible – we're all too different. It's about your attitude, how you respond.'

I frowned. 'Positive Mental Attitude – that's what I keep hearing about. But it sounds a bit stupid to me. Basically, you're saying that even if your house burns down and you lose everything, as long as you stay positive, it's alright.'

She shook her head. 'That's too simplistic. But I believe that when something bad happens you can either deal with it and move forward – even if that takes years – or become a victim of the event and carry it with you forever. Anything is only as powerful as the energy you allow it.' She sipped her juice. 'I'm not perfect, but I do make my own decisions.'

She made me wonder whether I do – suddenly the disjointed events that brought me to France appeared as links in a chain: the Decree Absolute, falling at school, the BMW driver, the argument with Jack. No matter how much I might have wished for a holiday I would never have taken one without Nicky intervening, and I'm only in Nice because I wanted to be like Meredith. Had I decided any of it?

'I can't work you out,' I said. 'Your situation with Marco and John is complicated, you're torn up about Savannah, you drink and do drugs – yet you're philosophical.' I smiled and shook my head. 'My life is dull, and I still can't find any answers.'

Meredith smiled too but looked away. 'I don't know. Maybe it was a big move at a young age that made me see a bigger picture. Maybe it's because my parents let me make mistakes. But please don't think I know something you don't. I've got no answers. I'm a mass of contradictions and my life is messy.'

'I don't think so. In fact, I admire the way

you juggle it. Even though I wouldn't do what you're doing, I'd like to have the guts to do it.'

'To do what?' Meredith's tone was sharp.

Taking a deep breath, I decided to tell her the lot. See what she thought. 'To take control. I want to go back to school. Get a law degree and a career I believe in, instead of stacking shelves for a few measly quid an hour.'

'So why don't you?' We had finished eating, and Meredith was filling the dishwasher. Then she poured more coffee and passed me a mug.

'How can I? Education is expensive, and I've got the boys to look after. It's too difficult.'

Lighting a cigarette, she took a drag and waved the smoke away from me. 'Nothing is impossible, Tana, and money is just a means to an end. How much do you want this? If you're serious about making changes, you'll figure it out.'

'That's easy for you to say. You have a wealthy husband.'

She frowned, flicked her ash. 'Can your parents help financially? Or could you get a loan? You're not even thirty – I don't know how long it takes but, worst case scenario, in ten years' time you could have a successful career. You'd have a long working life ahead of you.'

I brushed some crumbs from the table into my hand and threw them in the bin. 'I don't want to ask my parents for help and doubt any banks would lend to me. I don't earn much.'

'But you haven't asked! Surely that's the first step?'

I knew she was right but the thought of applying for a loan was scary. It would be the first step along the road I wanted to take, yet also worried might be a dead end. The number of things I would have to achieve, to create a new reality, made my stomach turn and my throat constrict. Part of me whispered that if I didn't try, I couldn't fail.

'Maybe. I don't know,' I said. 'I want so much for my life to be different – but the process feels overwhelming.'

Meredith put her feet up on the spare chair and drew deeply on her cigarette. 'Don't do anything then – don't ask, don't try. But when you're still stacking shelves and hating it on your fortieth birthday, don't blame me.'

'I know, but –'

'It's your choice.' She softened her tone and gave me a small smile. 'Tell me, when was the last time you did something that you really wanted to do, that was just for you?'

I looked out, into the garden, where the grass was lush and deep green, and the rosebushes bloomed with red and yellow flowers. The blue sky was dotted with puffy, white clouds. The colours were invigorating. Inspiring. I took a deep breath and blew it out hard. 'Last night,' I said. 'Up an alley with Stefan.'

She laughed, and her cigarette smoke

turned it into a choking cough. 'Well, that was a great introduction to the rest of your life.' Laughing again, she wiped her eyes. 'Ah man, that's funny.'

I laughed too. 'You know, I don't have many friends; I was so wrapped up in Jamie that I thought I didn't need them. I'm not great at trusting people, but you're different. You're honest.'

She smiled and leaned across the table to touch my hand. 'Thank you. I think you should start letting people in because you're missing out. That friend you mentioned – is it Nicky?' I nodded. 'She sounds great. You ought to spend more time with her. And seriously, do some investigation into how you could get a Law degree. You've already started making changes.'

Later we went to the beach, an expanse of pale pebbles that stretched as far as I could see. The sun woke my bones, and sprinkled the Mediterranean with winking, sparkling jewels. From my lounger I watched Meredith stride into the sea; she lifted her arms as she went deeper, delaying the moment of delicious surrender before sinking beneath the surface. She came back up with slick hair and a broad smile, beckoning me to join her.

I shook my head and lay back to scan the beach from behind my sunglasses. Family hubbub was everywhere, surrounding me with a familiar combination of parental chastisement, playing children and whinging toddlers. Mums were slathering sun cream onto wiggling children, teenagers were playing bat and ball at the water's edge, and tots were jumping over breaking ripples; it reminded me of trips to Cornwall when Jack was little. We would put in the hours at the beach building sandcastles and forts for him, or digging boats and cars out of the sand for him to play in. Jamie would go surfing and I'd watch.

It was a double-edged sword though; he was as fit and muscular as when we first met, whereas I was soft, stretched, scarred, and self-conscious. Every time we went, I wore a huge shirt over my swimsuit. My chest ached at the memory; I should have listened when Jamie said my baby weight was no big deal.

Sitting on my lounger, watching families interacting, I missed Jack and Oliver. I missed them as they are now, but also how they were when they were little. They are growing up so fast. When I'm low I focus on the negative aspects of motherhood but in truth those boys are the joys of my life, my reason for getting out of bed. I won't deny that the thought of childless freedom is dizzying – but I only feel that way when I'm tired, stressed, and feeling sorry for myself. I wouldn't swap.

Kids do drive their parents to distraction. It's kind of their job. All around me were countless children harassing their adults for time, attention, ice-cream – whatever they wanted right then – and mine are no different. I've heard it said that if you look for negatives you find them, but I realised that the same is true of positives, and I can't complain; everything I have is everything I created.

I have laid blame with my parents for living miles away and being unable to help me with childcare, with Jack for coming along too soon, with Oliver for keeping me up at night, and with Jamie for – well, I have blamed him for pretty much everything. But jealousy, blame and resentment are self-destructive. It's clear now.

By the time we got back from the beach I was desperate to speak to the boys, to tell them how much I love them and miss them. When I explained this to Meredith, she smiled and said that Nice has that effect.

Jamie's landline rang for a while but when Oliver finally answered, his gleeful 'Mummy!' made my heart throb. I wanted to pull him close and kiss him until he begged me to stop. He's my little man, the one thing I planned.

'How are you, Ollywobbles?' I asked, sitting myself on the stairs. 'What's been happening?'

He told me that Jamie had bought each of them a new BMX bike, even though Christmas and their birthdays are months away. A thorn of resentment pricked my heart. I took a few deep breaths though and pulled it out, focusing on changing my thoughts from negative to positive. In all fairness to Jamie, he doesn't get as much time with the boys as I do. It hurts that I cannot spoil them, but I should be grateful that he can. I told myself he didn't do it to spite me.

Jack came on the line next, sounding happy. He told me how cool their new bikes are and how he has put 'stunt nuts' on his back wheel. Oliver apparently stands on them, holding Jack's shoulders while he whizzes them around the park.

'You have to see us, Mum, we literally fly. It's so much fun. Olly was screaming.'

'Sounds amazing, darling,' I said, horrified. 'And where was Dad while this was happening?'

'Oh, he was there. He was filming it on his camcorder and laughing his head off.'

The stunt nuts sounded dangerous, and Jamie sounded irresponsible, but I bit my tongue because Jack sounded like himself, not the aggressive tyrant he's been lately. Regardless of my opinions about Jamie, he makes his children happy.

'He also bought us some of the limited-edition ones,' Jack went on. It took me a moment to realise he was now talking about some tiny, plastic pocket toys that are the latest craze.

'That's nice,' I said, thinking that they'll soon end up in the vacuum cleaner.

'I know, right? We've got twenty each now. They're really awesome. And really rare, so everyone at school will be *really* jealous. Dad's really generous.'

'Really?'

'Yeah. By the way, he wants to speak to you about something. See you soon Mum, bye!'

And he went, just like that. Caught in the moment, I juggled between speaking to Jamie or hanging up. But hanging up would be childish.

'Hello, Tana?' he said.

'Hi, Jamie, how are you?' I said, hoping to sound breezy and confident, nonchalant even. He could not know my hands were sweating and I wanted to be sick.

'Yeah, great thanks. I just wanted to tell you how much I'm enjoying having the boys here; it's been lots of fun. So, thanks.'

Was he being sarcastic? 'No problem. It helped me out. So, thank you, too.'

'Are you getting the break you wanted?'

'Well, not exactly, but it has been educational.'

'Oh,' he said. There was a short silence. 'That's … nice.'

'So, what did you want to talk to me about?' I wiped my wet palms on my legs and willed my heart to slow down – I was sure he'd be able to hear it pounding.

'Well, I wondered if you might want to go out for something to eat when you get back.' It sounded rehearsed. 'You know, the four of us. Just a pizza or something, nothing special. If you don't, no worries.' He coughed. 'But I want to see the boys more and thought it would be nice.'

I leaned back on the stairs, hardly believing it. The number of times I've wished for him to suggest going out as a family are countless. Although my head was whirling, I counted slowly to ten, giving the impression of considering his request.

'Yes, I guess so,' I said. 'I'd like that.' I took a deep breath. 'The boys would like it too. Let's sort something out when I get back.'

Relaying the conversation to Meredith ten minutes later, she cheered and held her hand up for a high five. 'Nice one!' she said. 'So, you're going to go out with him? I mean, them.'

'Yes, of course I am,' I said. 'It's what I've wanted ever since we split up. I know it's silly, but I was pig-headed and stubborn – I never wanted to split up in the first place.'

'You wanted him to beg.'

I shook my head. 'I'm an idiot. He did everything he could to not move out and not break up, but I wouldn't have it.'

'And he didn't beg, so you kept respecting him. Well done, Jamie.'

'Pretty much.' I looked at Meredith. 'You know, now we've both been with other people we're even. Going with Stefan felt like revenge, which is immature I know, but now I want to move on. If me and Jamie can be on good terms it'll be brilliant, for the boys' sake as well as my own.'

'Is that all you want, "good terms"?' Meredith raised her eyebrows and grinned.

'It's all I can hope for. The situation is so complicated.' I wasn't even sure what I meant by good terms, but I knew I wanted us to be friendly, or at least to be able to talk without animosity. 'We will never be together again,' I said. 'Too much has happened, there's too much emotion.'

'But you will go?' Meredith asked. 'You should.'

'Yes, but I'm already worrying about sitting at the same table as him! I love him, but haven't forgiven him – what if I get angry? Even worse, what if I cry?' I shook my head. 'Can you imagine?'

We were making dinner, just some chicken and salad, and Meredith laughed as she basted and turned the thigh pieces. Putting them back in the oven, she said, 'Yes, I can imagine. Absolutely. Remember, I have first-hand experience of how often you cry.'

'Bit rude.' I stopped slicing the tomatoes and held the knife up, grinning.

'I'm just joking.' She adjusted the oven temperature and reset the timer. 'I think you'll be ok. You said it yourself, you're even now. He's no worse than you. In fact, I reckon you're worse, because I doubt that he and Rose did it up an alley the second night they met.' She winked. 'Anyway, the boys will be there too, so you can focus your conversation on them. If it gets awkward, make an excuse, and cut the evening short.'

'Climb out the toilet window?'

She laughed again, showing her perfect teeth. 'Why not? Go for it.'

I finished making the salad, washed my hands, and admired my nails again. The boys would be surprised if they saw my manicure – I never usually decorate myself. Trying to imagine the four of us being like a family, I asked Meredith if she really thought it was a good idea to go out with them all, and said I thought it would be weird.

Meredith nodded. 'I do,' she said and squeezed my arm. 'It'll be fine, I'm sure. But if it's a disaster, you'll have your answer and won't do it again.'

The oven timer beeped; the chicken smelt amazing. I loaded our plates with salad and French bread, while she put the pan of roasted thighs on the table, and we sat down to eat.

'You have to go,' she said, popping a cucumber cube into her mouth. 'Nothing ventured, and all that.'

KATEBRAZIER

21

The weight of someone sitting down on the edge of my bed tugs at my stitches and wakes me. It is Meredith.

Illuminated by a path of light coming in from the corridor, she sits hunched forward, rubbing the back of her neck. The light reflects off her pale, wet cheeks, and her hair hangs lank and greasy. I make a noise in my throat.

'Tana!' she cries, shifting to face me, pulling all my stitches again. 'How are you? They called to say you'd woken up, but when I got here you were back asleep.' Lifting my hand, she squeezes gently. 'Oh my God, I'm so glad you're ok. You *are* ok, aren't you? Or is that a stupid question? I'm sorry, I can't think straight.'

I make another throaty noise and, realising I can't speak, she pulls a pad and pen from her bag.

'Can you write? Here, let's give it a go.'

She switches on the lamp and positions the pen in my hand, then rests my hand on top of the pad. It's painful but I can move my fingers enough to write, *what happened?*

'Oh Tana.' Her voice breaks. 'It was awful.

My fault entirely. I'm so sorry. I was stupid – you scared me to death. Do you remember anything?

No.

'Do you remember that door? I couldn't get it open. The catch was so slippery … all that blood, and you were … you were –' She buries her face in her hands, shoulders shaking as she sobs. 'I've never seen anything like it. I was so scared.'

Can't remember, I write.

Finally, she wipes her eyes and reads my words, then takes a deep breath. 'Ok, you need to know everything. I'll start from the beginning.'

She starts at Sunday evening, after we had been to the beach, and I'd spoken with Jamie about meeting for a pizza. Snippets come back – I remember we ate chicken and salad for dinner, and she said I should go out with Jamie and the boys.

She says we went clubbing again later, and a memory flickers, of leaving her house happy and laughing, glowing from the day's sunshine and my conversation with Jamie. Meredith admits she arranged another 'couples' night, so it was just us two, with Marco, and Stefan. It jangles a bell in my mind – I think I'd considered having another go with Stefan if he seemed up for it.

As she talks, walking to the club comes back to me. I remember the three of them having a heated discussion which Meredith translated; she wanted to go to the club we'd been at the night before, the neon palace with foam and things, but the guys vetoed it. I didn't get a say either way. Stefan lit a Marlborough and pulled a tiny package, like a doll's envelope, out of the cigarette box. He showed Meredith and asked her something, nodding towards me.

I had no idea what the little package was, but she snapped at him and shook her head. He mumbled '*pardon*' and held his hands up, then slipped it back into his pocket. Meredith glared at him, grabbed my hand, and pulled me to walk in front of them.

'What the hell was that about? What's Stefan done?'

'Nothing,' she said. 'But he forgets that not everybody does drugs. I didn't want him waving them about in your face.'

'What was it? More weed?'

'No.' She lit a cigarette, and the smoke smelt unusually sweet in the evening air. 'It's probably cocaine, knowing Stefan. But it could be something else; he likes to mix it up a bit.'

A thousand butterflies fluttered in my stomach. At school they had drummed into us the dangers of drugs, and although I knew loads of kids back then who took acid, cocaine was another league. I wiped my prickling palms on my jeans.

'Do you do it too? I thought it was dangerous.'

'It's fine,' she said. 'And yeah, I do it when I'm here. When we go out it puts everyone in a good mood and lets us drink more.'

So that's how they drank so much. I figured it was why she had been sniffing so much too, on Friday night. 'What does it feel like?'

The roads were quiet, and the sky was darkening. Meredith stopped beneath a streetlight. She looked at me with wide eyes, a smile pulling up one corner of her mouth.

'I've never met anyone who has never tried anything before,' she said. Frowning, as if she were inspecting an unidentified creature, she bit her lip, tilted her head. 'It's amazing.'

Feeling foolish, I shrugged. 'What can I say? My school ingrained in us that we'd drop dead if we tried drugs or, best case, be junkies forever. They scared the hell out of me! Then I got pregnant with Jack, so that was that. I was hardly going to start dabbling then, was I?'

Meredith shook her head. 'No, of course not. I wasn't having a go at you. It's just a novelty, having to explain it all.'

Stefan and Marco caught up with us and we carried on walking into town. The sky got darker, there were no stars, and the air smelt of impending rain. Meredith and Marco were holding hands but neither Stefan nor I made a similar move – my mind was elsewhere, trying to decide about the cocaine. I wanted to try everything I had missed but was scared.

'Meredith.' I touched her arm. 'Can I try some?'

She squinted at me in the low light. 'What, coke? You're kidding, right?'

'No,' I said, shaking my head. 'I can't explain but I really want to. A little bit can't hurt, can it?'

She studied me, one hand on her hip, deep grooves corrugating her forehead, then shrugged and said, 'I guess not. I'll sort it out when we get inside.'

'Thanks.'

'Just a bit though, to see what you think.'

A few minutes later, we stopped at some bollards which blocked access to a narrow, cobbled street. It was packed with people.

'We're here now,' Meredith said. 'The entrance is down there.'

She pointed into the gloom, and I stood on tiptoes to try and see, but could only make out a sea of heads, a red sign flashing the name of the club, and a couple of weak streetlights. Muffled bass rose and fell, presumably as the bouncers allowed people in. We joined the end of the queue, and as the line shuffled slowly towards the entrance, it started raining. My shirt became damp and chilly, and I hugged myself, wishing we could go back to the neon palace from the night before.

'It looks like a right dive,' I said, thinking that a queue for Hades' Underworld might look similar.

'Oh, it is.' Meredith sighed. 'It's totally seedy.

But Stefan likes the music – there's no pop in this place. Plus, they don't take much notice of what everyone's up to, if you get what I mean.' She held a finger beneath her nose and did an exaggerated sniff.

My stomach churned as we shuffled closer to the bouncers; with each opening of the door came a belch of chaotic noise. I hugged myself tighter, took deep breaths and kicked the cobblestones, persuading myself that this was a night to tick off my 'Live a Little' list, but by the time they opened the door for us, I was already regretting it.

Heat and darkness assaulted us first. The air inside was a thick, murky, stinking fug of sweat, smoke machines and alcohol – cut only by dazzling strobes which made those dancing twitch and jerk. The boys headed straight to the bar, but the roaring, formless bass and fast, high-end blasts which constituted music froze me on the threshold. It sliced my skin and clawed my organs. No melodies or lyrics. No chance of a last dance love song at the end of this night.

Meredith pointed into the gloom and shouted, 'We sit over there, at the back.' She grabbed my hand and led me across the crowded dance floor to their usual table and sofas, said she would be back in five, and disappeared to the toilets.

The guys came back from the bar and Stefan smiled as he handed me a lurid pink drink. They sat at the low table, pulled out their little wraps and began chopping lines.

I stood, sipping my glass of bubbles, and taking in the stained, threadbare sofas, the way my shoes stuck to the floor. Imagining the bacteria embedded into every surface, not to mention the drug residue, I shuddered. The place was one huge pathogen. Where were the fire exits? Where were the windows?

Every inch of me recoiled, but I put on a smile and bobbed with the bassline, figuring that if a quiet evening with hot chocolate and a book wasn't an option, I should join in. A few more glasses of that sweet, delicious fizziness, and I would be ok.

When she came back, Meredith was even more vivacious and animated than usual. Her eyes were sparklers, her mouth had too many words. I was envious. If nothing else, that magic powder would stop me worrying about bugs in the soft furnishings. Beckoning her over, I asked again if I could try it.

'Are you sure?' she said. 'It's strong.' I nodded. She shrugged. 'Come on then.'

The cocktail and the dark, foggy club with its repetitive music, transported me as we navigated the crowded dance floor. My head was crooked. It felt like I was merging with everyone else, assimilating, losing myself. Repulsion was sliding into acceptance.

I can't explain wanting to try cocaine,

it goes against everything I believe in; my only justification is mental metamorphosis. My shackles of judgement were loosening. If the others were ok taking it, where was the harm? Why shouldn't I do something crazy and irresponsible, just for once?

Meredith and I squeezed into a tiny toilet cubicle where the floor and seat were wet, there was no tissue, and the bowl was stained. Graffiti I couldn't read covered the walls, but the drawings and phone numbers were clear enough. I held my breath and stood on tiptoe.

Meredith glanced at my face and laughed. 'Gross, right?'

'Unbelievable,' I said. 'I wish I had my wet wipes. Don't these women have any self-respect?'

She laughed. 'People don't come here for the facilities.' Pulling a packet of tissues from her bag, she closed the seat and wiped it over. 'We're lucky there's a lid.'

Watching Meredith's ritual was fascinating. She squatted beside the toilet, wobbling slightly on the balls of her feet, and opened a tiny envelope like Stefan's. If I did it my hands would shake, and I'd drop the lot into the puddle on the floor, but her hands were steady. She tapped a small pile of white powder onto the lid and chopped it finer, using the side of her bank card. With quick, precise movements she drew the pile downwards into thin lines, and in a matter of seconds, one was waiting for me.

'There you go.'

My heart was racing, my palms felt sticky. Meredith had warned that the coke was strong, and I was frightened of having one sniff and being hooked for life. I hate drugs, always have since they made my friends act weird when we were young, yet I still wanted to try. Looking at Meredith, knowing she enjoyed them recreationally, I figured it would be alright. Repressed Tana said *do it*. I clenched my fists and took a deep breath.

'Cool. Thanks.' I didn't move.

Meredith frowned. 'Tana, are you sure, you're sure? You look like a ghost.'

'I am sure,' I said, nodding. 'But I don't know what to do.' I laughed and she quickly covered the line to stop my breath blowing it away.

'It's easy. Here, take this.' She handed me a rolled ten Euro note. 'Stick that up your nose and close the other nostril with your finger. Sniff as hard as you can, moving the note up the line.' She mimed the process.

It sounded easy enough. Squatting down, I pushed aside all thoughts of bacteria, stuck the note up my nose, and in one swift sniff, snorted the powder.

It was horrible.

The crystals were chopped fine but felt as big as sugar cubes, and they smelt terrible, like rotting vegetables. Within seconds my nostril was blocked, then it went numb.

'Rub that last bit round your gums,' Meredith said, and when I did, my front teeth went numb too.

Sniffing and wiping could not stop my nose running. My face was rubbery, like I'd had a shot of novocaine; my lips felt swollen. A thick mixture of cocaine and snot suddenly ran down the back of my throat, numbing there too.

'Are you ok?' Meredith's eyes danced with amusement.

'It's repulsive,' I gasped, holding my throat and gagging. 'Why would you take this stuff?'

She smiled. 'That's normal. It'll soon pass, and you'll want more.'

'I doubt it. It's fucking disgusting.'

'Just wait.'

I stood aside so she could take the other line. Meredith's was long and thick, twice the size of mine, but she bent and sniffed like an expert, stopping halfway to switch nostrils. Afterwards she stood and looked at me with wide eyes, wrinkling her nose, then quickly wiped beneath it. Wasting no time, she ran her finger over the toilet seat to collect any leftovers and scrubbed it into her teeth and gums.

'Ugh,' I said. 'That is grim.'

She grinned. 'Waste not, want not.'

I felt filthy. I couldn't bear to think about what we had sniffed up with the coke, but Meredith acted as if it were totally normal. She showed no reaction to having taken that big, fat line – she wasn't retching like me. My throat, jaw and cheek were numb, and my nose felt blocked, yet no amount of sniffing could stop it from running.

Meredith patted her cheeks and did some strange facial yoga. 'Gotta make sure everything's working,' she said, shaking her head. Her hair shimmied down her back. 'You ready to go back in?'

I had almost forgotten about the boys waiting for us in the club; it felt like we'd been in that rank little toilet for hours. Nodding, I wiped my hand under my nose again, marvelling at its rubbery feel. It reminded me of a nose / glasses / moustache combo that Mum bought me when I was six; I had seen it in the toy shop window and pleaded, thinking if I wore it nobody would know who I was. After Meredith licked the edge of her bank card and packed everything into her bag, I led the way back through the crowded club, feeling like that six-year-old again.

The cocaine experience was not one of hyperactivity like I had imagined, but my senses were sharpened. Wide awake and hyper alert, unfamiliar confidence hijacked my usual self-consciousness, and I held my head high as we strode through the clubbers. I met Marco and Stefan with a broad smile, and sitting beside Meredith I ignored all implications of the stained, sticky seats.

We talked at top speed, witty and insightful;

we had the answers to all problems. We were funny and interesting. My quips and anecdotes had Meredith roaring with laughter, and I felt special, with a million relevant things to say. My thoughts turned briefly to Jamie; if he had called me right then, I would have had no qualms about chatting.

Turning to Stefan and Marco, the limited French I remembered from school was no obstacle to communication and we created beautiful linguistic patterns, incomprehensible to anyone else. The four of us laughed and talked, gesticulating wildly to embellish our words, compulsively sniffing, and wiping our noses. We bought round after round of drinks, which disappeared quickly but didn't seem to affect us at all.

Meredith was right though – within an hour I was irritated and antsy, my fingers playing cat's cradle without any string; I wanted more magic powder. The craving was persistent. After twitching for a while, I offered her money for another line.

In a cubicle even dirtier than the first one, the process of chopping and snorting no longer felt like the lowest point to which I could stoop. It was more like belonging to an exclusive club. I asked for a bigger line and, watching her chop it, felt my heart beating erratically. My armpits were damp, and my scalp felt tight. My shirt stuck to my back.

'Is that ok for you?' Meredith asked, leaning aside. Two long, fat lines lay side by side on the lid.

'That's awesome.' I squatted down and pressed my unblocked nostril.

She handed me the note.

22

My memory is blank after that.

The hospital ward is quiet and Meredith's sobs echo. So far, her story has been more like a confession and my memories have been just one step behind, but now she stops and all I can do is wait.

'And so,' she says, wiping her eyes, 'you took that bigger line. I knew it was too much. I knew it was too strong.' She looks again at the hole in my throat, the wires and machines, and fresh tears run down her cheeks. 'I'm so sorry, Tana. Look at the state of you. I should have said no.'

I asked for it, I write.

'I know, but even so … I should have stopped you. Do you remember what happened next?'

No.

'We had those fat ones and then I split the last little bit between us. It was hardly anything, but you'd had too much already. When I looked up, you'd gone all weird.' She stares at the curtains, seeing the club toilet cubicle. Her wet cheeks shine.

I'm not sure what she means, so write a question mark on the pad.

'It's hard to explain. You went kind of … blank. You needed help, but that fucking door wouldn't open. The lock kept slipping.' She hangs her head and wrings her hands. 'I'm so sorry.'

Something clicks in my mind. Shutting my eyes, I force myself to remember.

Pounding bass rattles the cubicle walls. The wet floor is littered with wads of stained tissue and a used condom. Meredith and I are squished in; she is squatting beside the toilet, making two large lines on the lid, and I am watching, trying to ignore my erratic heartbeat and sweaty skin. My scalp feels tight, but I figure all these things must be normal side effects of the coke wearing off.

Looking up, she smiles at me. 'You like it then?' I nod and she turns back to her chopping. 'Are you sure you want this much, Tana? It's strong stuff. Stefan gets it from a guy he's known for years. He barely cuts it.'

I say yes and she leans aside. 'Is that ok for you?'

'That's awesome.'

She hands me the note.

Sniffing hard, I do the lot and within seconds the caustic powder hits the back of my nose and slides down my throat, making me retch again. Meredith smirks.

'Oh, that's gross.' I wipe my stinging eyes and raise what must be the sixth or seventh lurid pink drink of the night. 'It's a good job I brought this to wash it down. Cheers!'

Meredith laughs and pretends to clink my glass with her imaginary one. 'Cheers.'

Gulping the cocktail, I lean against the cubicle wall and watch her sniff her line. Her hair looks so pretty spread across her back, incongruous with the filthy place and sordid actions.

'I would never have imagined us together, doing this,' I say. 'Not in a million years.'

She sits back on her heels, wipes her nose and sniffs, then dabs her finger into the residue and rubs it over her gums. 'Yeah, it's weird. And not in a million years would I have imagined that you'd be into random sex and drugs.' Her face contorts as the powder hits the back of her throat and, with an involuntary shiver, she indicates the dusting of powder left. 'Here, you have that last bit.'

I can't feel my nose, tongue or lips but don't want to waste anything, so dab the last of it and rub inside my mouth. 'It's all a one-off. Your bad influence.' A rush of saliva fills my mouth, and I swallow, making my throat even more numb.

Meredith's mouth smiles but her eyes don't.

'Hey, I'm joking,' I say. 'Everything this weekend has been my choice.' My nose is running again, despite the feeling of it being plugged with concrete. 'I know this isn't what I came away for, but it's been fun trying new things. I've let loose. Honestly, I'm having a blast.'

'The thing is, Tana, I'd rather be like you.'

My nose is aching now, and the club sounds are muffled. I can hear a high-pitched whine. My heart feels loose. 'You're kidding, right?'

She shakes her head. 'I'm not. You take life seriously and worry about doing things properly.'

'Yeah, I'm boring. Don't rub it in.' I try to focus on my breathing.

'No, you're not.' Meredith smears some gloss on her lips and rubs them together. 'I thought sensible meant boring, but it just means cautious. I'm the opposite; I jump blindly into anything that looks like fun. It's stupid.'

'It's better than being vanilla.' The whining sound is irritating, but rubbing my ears makes it louder. I feel sick and my vision keeps blurring.

'Not really.' Meredith looks sad.

Suddenly, I'm not excited anymore. My ears and nose are blocked. My face is rubber. The walls are slanting. 'All I do is shout at my kids. I'm no fun.'

Meredith flushes her empty cocaine wrap, packs away her card and the rolled-up note, then sits on the toilet. Crossing her legs, she lights a cigarette. 'We all lose control. At least you recognise it.'

The cubicle seems to be collapsing in on us and the air is thick. Leaning against the wall as my vision blurs, it's like I'm breathing through a straw.

The whining gets louder, and I clutch my head and ask Meredith if she can hear it, but she just looks confused. I need to get out of here. I need to breathe. I need to feel rain on my face. My heart is pounding, and someone is shouting, banging on our cubicle door, over and over.

'They want us to hurry up,' Meredith says, and shouts back at them – but she doesn't move.

I'm scared. I'm sweating all over, my muscles are jittery, and my hands keep trembling. My nose, teeth, and throat are numb, my face is a mask. Words won't come. I'm dizzy. All the edges look soft. Snot dribbles into my mouth.

Closing my eyes to fight the vertigo, I brace myself against the shrinking cubicle and gulp for air, but my heartbeat is still erratic. When I touch my nose, my fingers get smeared with blood.

Why is my nose bleeding?

I can't stand straight, everything is whirling, and I need Meredith's help, but she is digging about in her bag and doesn't know.

A gush of blood fills my mouth and nose, it runs down my throat. Spitting it out, I watch bright crimson life spray the cubicle walls and splash down my white shirt. I'm trying to grab the door lock, but my hands are flapping and blood splatters over the door, the walls, and floor.

Turning, I grab Meredith's arm, and she looks up and screams. 'What the fuck happened?'

Red mist sprays in her face as I try and

speak. She pushes me aside and her arms and hands are everywhere – she is trying to get out and I need to get out too; there's no air in here, but the door won't open.

Now it's Meredith hollering and banging on the door; she's screaming for help and wrestling with the lock, but her hands are now covered in blood – my blood – and they keep slipping. She is yanking and twisting but even though it worked just fine to lock us in here, it won't let us out.

I need to sit. I need air. Breathing is hard. Everything is sideways. Has someone turned down the lights? The bass is quieter – they're just playing that high pitched whine. I grab my head and squeeze, but the noise won't stop.

My heart slows.

I'm so tired.

Can't keep my eyes open.

Why is Meredith frantic?

Slipping to the floor between the toilet and the wall soaks my jeans with other people's piss. It all goes quiet. Meredith's mascara is smudged down her cheeks. Her mouth is moving but I can't hear her. Just the high-pitched whining.

She kicks the cubicle door. It rattles but doesn't open. She grabs my head and tilts it, yells in my face. Her hands get bloodier.

Everything is fine – what's her problem? I want to say it's ok, that I'm calm, but I can't speak. My arms and legs are frozen. The taste of iron fills my mouth, and blood runs down my throat. I gag and cough. There is no air.

Resting my head on the toilet, I watch Meredith slap and kick the door. High-pitched buzzing fills my ears.

A woman's head and shoulders appear at the top of the door, miles away. She moves in slow motion. She is blurry. She shouldn't lean over the door like that. She could fall. Her hair swings from her upside-down head.

Soft.

I want to grab it, but my arm won't move. The woman twists the catch, the door unlocks. She disappears then she is holding the door open. Why does she look so angry? Shaking her head at me, she leaves.

A sour, metallic blood bubble pops on my mouth. More and more come. They are so pretty, so bright, and when they pop, more thin, red mist sprays into the thick air.

Meredith is crying. She looks a mess, with blood all over her hands and mascara all down her face. She usually looks so nice.

Why is she pulling and yanking me about, shouting words I can't understand? They make no sense over the rushing and whining. I wish she'd leave me alone.

I can't get up, I'm too tired. My limbs don't work. I'm fine on the floor – I'll just watch. My heart has stopped galloping. That's good.

Thoughts come and go, like fluttering leaves on a breeze, slowly, slowly, falling, turning. I want to sleep. But Meredith won't let me.

Don't move me. Stop pulling. Stop tugging. I shut my eyes; she slaps my face. I'm tipping. She tries to lift me.

Stop it.

I can't feel.

Let me sleep.

Meredith looks wild. Blood stains her hands and face. Even her hair. She yells at everyone who comes into the toilet, and they stare at me, shake their heads.

Panting and crying, she heaves me up and holds my arm across her shoulder. She wraps her arm around my waist.

My legs are weak, but she is strong. Barging the door open, she walks me through the club. My feet, miles below, shuffle along. The place is packed, and people are high. Nobody looks at me. The door moves further away.

When we get near, Meredith shouts at the bouncers. They look at me, then each other. One rolls his eyes and holds the door open, the other gets his phone out.

Cool, fresh air rushes in, rejuvenating me enough to break free from Meredith's grasp. I stagger out into the narrow street, but the cobblestones are slick with rain and my feet slip, my knees buckle. The world turns sideways. I am spiralling and twisting. Falling. The ground rushes up and my head cracks the cobbles, stone against bone.

   Laying on wet ground, I have no energy to move. There is no air.

23

Meredith hands me a tissue. 'Do you remember now?'

Kind of, I scribble. But really, after falling, I have nothing. *What then?*

She presses her palms together and holds them to her mouth, her eyes filled with sadness. After a deep sigh, she says, 'Those bouncers called an ambulance but wouldn't help any more than that. They just shrugged and said it was your own fault.'

She shakes her head, looking so miserable I want to hug her.

Why am I so hurt?

'After you slipped and bashed your head,' she whispers, 'you wouldn't respond.' It's a strain to hear her. 'Nobody would help me.' Charcoal smudges sit beneath Meredith's liquid eyes. Her mouth is flat, and she is wringing her hands.

'I didn't know what to do. It was horrible. You weren't breathing ... I couldn't make you breathe. I was shaking you and banging on your chest, but nothing worked.' Wiping tears away, she says, 'You were all floppy and heavy. I don't know first aid – I just copied what they do on TV.

I think I broke your ribs. I'm so sorry.'

I wasn't breathing?

Meredith shakes her head. 'No. Your mouth and nose were full of blood.'

This is a huge amount to take in. My life could have ended with a cocaine overdose in a grimy backstreet club, and that's what people would remember of me. Where would that have left Jack and Oliver? My ribs are the last things I'm worried about.

I almost died?

'Yes. And it's my fault.' Meredith breaks into fresh sobs.

Unbelievable. I expected bad, but not horrendous. *It's ok re ribs*, I write.

Her face contorts as tears drip from her chin, and her breath comes in short gasps. 'It's not, Tana. I feel so bad – I hurt you even more.'

Accidentally.

'I know,' she says, with a thin smile, 'but I still feel terrible. Shall I carry on?'

There's more?

She presses her lips together and nods. 'It isn't pretty.'

None of this is. Watching Meredith as she wipes her face and tries to calm her breathing, no doubt deciding how to drop the next bombshell, I feel sorry for her. This is all my fault – I turned her fun week into a nightmare, and don't know how I can ever make amends. She looks drawn and exhausted, her clothes are wrinkled, and I wonder how many hours she sat by my bedside while I slept.

'The ambulance was quick,' she says at last, 'and the paramedics were brilliant. But it was your heart, Tana – your heart stopped.'

What?!

'I know it's a lot to deal with, but I need to tell you.' Her words are rushed, like she does not want them in her mouth for long. 'They parked by those bollards and ran down to us, but by the time they took over from me doing CPR, you hadn't breathed for a few minutes. It felt like hours.' She meets my eyes. 'I know – it was terrifying. They used a defibrillator to shock your heart.'

My pen scratches on the paper: *What the fuck?*

'Honestly, Tana,' she says, 'it was so scary. They got your heart beating again but there was so much blood in your nose and throat that you still couldn't breathe. There was no suction machine on the ambulance – they can't carry everything – so ...'

What?

'Well, the hospital is a fifteen-minute drive from the club.'

And?

Her pained expression says she's exasperated and wants me to work it out for myself, but I can't. My mind is empty.

'So, you'd already not breathed for a few

minutes. Another fifteen … you'd have died. So, the paramedics operated. They gave you a tracheotomy. Do you know what that is?'

Shutting my eyes in acknowledgement, tears wet my cheeks. I knew it.

'It was an emergency – they had to do something.' Her voice breaks. Pressing clenched fists against her mouth, her eyes echo with inexpressible guilt. 'The doctor says you need another small operation to remove it and close the hole.'

Great.

What on earth was I doing, taking drugs? Did I expect no repercussions, having not taken anything before? Why didn't I think about possible consequences – why didn't I think about my sons?

Right now, I hate myself more than I ever thought possible. Whenever I look in the mirror, I will be reminded of how I almost lost my life and how my boys almost lost their mum, for the sake of a night out.

We sit silently for a while. Meredith is picking at a thread on her top and I'm trying to absorb everything. The gaps have been filled but why I reacted so badly remains incomprehensible. There are so many questions. One keeps niggling so I write it on the pad.

'Wednesday,' she says.

I've been here three days? In a coma?

She shakes her head. 'Not exactly. They

sedated you for the first 48 hours. You needed detoxification, so they gave you a blood transfusion, you know, to make sure all the drugs were out of your system and ensure your kidneys and liver and everything had minimal damage. Also, because you smacked your head when you fell, they did a load of scans to make sure you didn't fracture your skull or facial bones.'

Did I?

She smiles and shakes her head. 'No. You're all good. You must have an iron skull because you should've heard the noise when you whacked the ground. I heard it over the music. But thankfully, it's fine. They've stitched the cut on your forehead.' Meredith's eyes are wide, honest. 'I have never been so relieved, as when they told me you're alive and your head's ok. I was terrified, Tana. What happened in those toilets is the most frightening thing I've ever experienced.'

It's not exactly great for me either, but what frightens me most, is that had any link in the chain of people who came together to save me been broken, I'd be dead.

Not here, dead.

That's forever.

If there had been roadworks or an accident to delay the ambulance, if Meredith had not dragged me out of that toilet as quickly as she did, if the paramedics had not been so skilled ...

if, if, if. If they hadn't been so proactive and professional, if the nurses and consultant hadn't been so thorough ... they all played their part in saving my life. Even those ignorant bouncers who called the ambulance did something, albeit reluctantly. If they had not helped me just in time, the alternative doesn't bear thinking about.

Meredith holds my hand between hers. She can barely look me in the eye, but she has nothing to feel bad about. I'm the stupid, guilty one. My boys are at home in England, and I am hundreds of miles away in a hospital bed. I can hardly move, I have a tracheotomy tube in my throat, and I'm wired up to drips, tubes and monitors because I almost died, trying to grab a slice of the life I thought I'd missed.

What an idiot I am. How pathetic I feel. What a selfish, juvenile thing to have done. With every minute that passes, I loathe myself more.

'I went with you in the ambulance, and I've been here most of the time you've been sleeping,' Meredith says. It's clear that she needs to talk about what happened. 'Marco, Stefan and the girls came with me too.' She indicates the bedside table. 'They brought you some stuff.'

I smile. *Thanks.*

'It was the least I could do.'

Sitting quietly for a few moments, Meredith looks like she is trying to work out whether to say something more. She keeps looking at her hands and massaging her wrist with her thumb, then looking at me indecisively.

'Tana,' she says at last, 'really, we're all mortified. Stefan is devastated – he's the one who bought the coke. Obviously, he can't get a refund or make a complaint, but he says he'll tell the guy he got it from what happened to you.'

No point, I write.

'No, probably not,' she says, rubbing her arm, self-soothing. 'But he should be told. Anyway, none of us will take it again.'

I don't know why I did. I hate drugs.

Meredith nods. 'Me too, now I've seen what can happen. You scared the life out of me.'

She adjusts her position on the bed and my ribs protest. 'I did tell that consultant what you took, but there wasn't any left for him to analyse – I flushed my wrap away and the boys did all theirs too. He reckons it could've been cut with anything – rat poison, bleach, anything white to bulk it.' She shakes her head. 'I guess I was wrong about it not being cut much. Or maybe it was really pure. Either way, that dealer doesn't care about the risk; he just wants maximum profit.'

You guys were all ok.

'I know, that's what's weird. They took blood from me, Marco, and Stefan because we'd all had it, but thankfully we were fine. The tests came back normal.' She shrugs. 'But that's why they did so many on you – you know, to see whether you've got some sort of sensitivity. They were trying to work out if there's an underlying reason why you reacted so badly.'

Is there?

'I don't know. The doctor said something about tolerance.'

This just gets better and better. What could have caused my reaction? Maybe an undiagnosed heart condition? I want Meredith to translate everything because I need to know exactly what they've done to me, why, and what they found. First though, there's something else I need to know.

Do my boys know I'm here?

Meredith nods slowly, and fiddles with her earring. 'I contacted Jamie through Facebook – he had to know. I'm sorry if that was the wrong thing to do, but if it was me, I'd want my family with me.'

To my surprise, I feel relieved. *It was the right thing*, I write.

She smiles. 'Oh good. I was worried you'd be angry. I didn't go into any detail, I promise. I just said you'd had a weird turn and fallen and banged your head.'

Sounds dodgy, I write. *What did he say?*

'He wanted to come straight over. They would have got on the first flight, but I explained that they were keeping you sedated, that it might be better to wait a day or two. I've kept him updated though; I rang him earlier to say you were awake.'

Thank you.

She looks at me and smiles thinly. 'He really cares about you, Tana. I mean, I know you've been through some tough times, and you think he hates you, but he doesn't. No way. He's been worried. I really think there's a chance for you two.'

I can't get drawn into that conversation. It's too complicated and emotional and I'd need my voice. But it's food for thought. *My parents?* I write.

'Jamie got in touch with them. Don't roll your eyes, he had to, didn't he? I'd have done the same and so would you. I don't know how much he's told them, but they know you're here.'

Oh God, my parents. They'll want an explanation, but the truth will push them over the edge. They're too old for that kind of shock; I'll have to invent a plausible lie.

I wonder if anyone else knows. It's important to me that nobody else ever finds out what I did. The whole thing was a stupid mistake, and I can't have rumours rippling through the school community. I feel sick just thinking about it. Meredith must never tell anyone because the mums would gossip, and my boys would never live it down.

I also wonder what Jamie said, what he thought, when Meredith called him. He must have been confused by her vague story of me falling. How did he feel when she told him I was awake? Was he relieved? Will he come over? So many questions.

I'm exhausted. The knowledge has burdened, wizened, shrunken me. Flying to France last Friday, planning to rest and recharge, seems a decade ago. Too much has happened. I need to process it, but it will take time, and right now I can barely keep my eyes open.

Meredith realises. She puts the pad and pen on the table and shoulders her bag. 'You need to sleep,' she says. 'I'll go now.' Squeezing my hand again, she whispers, 'See you tomorrow.'

24

I've been nil by mouth for four days now, so the smells of toast and coffee wafting into my room are almost too much to bear. When I can eat again, I'll savour every taste and texture. When I can drink again, I'll appreciate the sensation. This is my promise.

From this moment I will value everything, even the boring things I used to whinge about: housework, supermarket work, arguing children. They are calling me. The change I craved, the excitement I imagined – none of it was real. Give me normal. Give me mundane, give me monotony. Just give me my life.

The consultant arrives with a beaming smile, and a translator to explain what they did and what they found. The team here saved me, and I will be forever grateful, but can hardly bear to meet their eyes because although they are kind and professional, it's a bit like being reprimanded by a head teacher. They don't see me; they see a fool who did something reckless and irrational. Despite wishing that I could tell them I'm a good person and a good mum who simply had a moment of madness, I can only listen. Mute.

Progress is good, I am told, but I need one more brain scan. That doesn't faze me – the clarity of last night's memories tells me that my brain is functioning fine. They will also remove the tube today so, hopefully, I will be free to leave on Saturday.

Why did I react so badly? I write.

The translator asks and the consultant shrugs, pressing his lips together and shaking his head. They speak rapidly, then the translator says Meredith told them I had never taken any drugs before, and that the cocaine was strong. So, it must have been some kind of allergic reaction – certainly a massive shock to my system.

What about my heart?

They assure me it is fine.

I also ask if they can leave the tube in my throat because I don't want another operation, but the response is definitive: *'Non.'* The operation is simple, they say. Quick. Minor. I'll be fine.

But my stomach is fluttering. The thought of anaesthetic terrifies me. It was a struggle to wake up after losing three whole days locked in darkness, and I don't want to go under again. What happens to consciousness when you're out cold like that? Where do "you" go? It's not like being asleep. Under anaesthetic, there is no peripheral awareness or dream state, no vague sense of warmth or cold or sound. It's just a yawning chasm of nothingness.

In contrast, the midday sunshine has warmed my bedsheets, and my little room feels cosy. I don't want to go anywhere. Besides, I've only just begun my recovery – what if more drugs in my system pushes me backwards? Not to mention that there's nobody here for me, except Meredith. I don't want to go through waking up again to such crushing loneliness.

What if it takes me ages to wake?

What if I don't wake?

Statistically, lots of errors happen, even during routine operations. Anaesthetic is risky.

What if something goes wrong and I die here, all alone? The thought makes me sweat but, in my heart, I know there's no alternative. It's time for big girl pants. This revolting tube must come out.

A nurse checks all my drips and monitors, then two porters arrive. They steer my bed past the nurses' station, into the lift and through a maze of corridors downstairs. The hospital is busy, and people stare as we pass, probably wondering what's wrong with me and where we're going. It's like they are parading me, to show as many bystanders as possible what happens when you overdose.

Eventually, we push through a pair of heavy doors into the operating theatre, where a team is busy, preparing the equipment. So much fuss, just for me. An enormous, circular light hovers over the table like a spaceship. In this alien environment, I am their specimen. The surgeon speaks to a nurse, who nods and shows him some charts. He barely looks at me; I am simply number whatever on his agenda for today.

Managing to catch his eye, I offer a weak smile, thinking, please, please, look after me. I have two young boys. Please keep me safe.

His mouth flicks upwards but it is impersonal, and I know I am nothing more than a piece of meat to him. Suddenly though, I see that my life has meaning; I have family, friends, and children.

They hold the mask to my face. Please don't make any ...

Voices.
Whose?
Eyelids ... heavy ...
Man. Jamie?
Jamie?
Are the boys? ... I can't ... tired.

Someone is here. Next to me – Jamie? A touch on my hand, hesitant but familiar. Quick shallow breaths and sniffs ... crying?

Sounds again, clearer, stronger. Finally, I can keep my eyes open. I'm more alert, can think more clearly, but am alone. I was sure that Jamie was here, sitting by my bed. It seemed so real.

The curtains are open, and the sky is the glorious, rich blue of late summer. A high-flying plane leaves a wide, white swash behind. I am groggy, and my throat is sore, but I am breathing for myself. That hideous piece of metal is gone.

Footsteps approach, light and quick. I think it's the nurse or maybe Meredith, but then there's more than one pair and they're running, and there's giggling. A man calls a warning.

Jamie. Jack. Oliver.

Oh, my goodness. It's too soon.

I should be delighted to hear their footsteps, to realise they love me and are here because they're worried – but I'm not. I can't face them. Not yet.

It's paradoxical: I'm desperate to see them yet frightened of reality. Cuddling the boys and catching up on their news will burst the bubble. I need longer to digest everything – I need time to get strong. Facing the three of them right now, when I've been laid up for days and still feel broken, is too much.

But they are approaching fast and there is nowhere to hide, barely time to think. My brain is fuzzy; I don't know what to do or how to be.

Oliver skids to a halt in the doorway and shouts, 'Mummy!'

I shut my eyes and don't react.

'Go in!' says Jack.

'Don't push me!'

'Well don't tell me what to do.'

Nothing's changed with them, then.

Jamie catches up in a few strides and tells the boys to go in. 'It's alright, Oliver,' he says quietly. 'Mummy's sleeping. She's had an operation and is very tired.'

'But why does she look all funny?' Oliver asks. 'Why is she cut? Why is her face all purple? What are those bags for? Why is that tube going into her arm?'

Oliver is only seven. He has never seen anyone in hospital. Meredith said I had stitches in my forehead, and I assume my face is battered and bruised. Maybe it's swollen. Either way, he is upset, and I don't think Jamie should have brought him. Nor Jack. The boys should not see me like this.

Yet pretending to sleep is harder than anticipated. I feel ridiculous. Listening to every word, I can picture every facial expression. Guilt says I should have a conversation, but I honestly cannot deal with them all right now. As awful as it sounds, I would prefer for Meredith to be here.

'Daddy, what's in that bag?' Oliver is breathing by my ear, and I know he is frowning, that his tongue is sticking out as he goes up on tiptoes and stretches, trying to touch the dangling pouch of fluid.

'It's just some special water. Mummy needs it because she can't drink by herself at the moment. She'll be back to normal soon though, don't you worry.'

'But what's that black stuff? Will that go away too?'

'That's called stitching; you know, like when you get a hole in your sock.' Jamie sounds uncertain, so I must look bad. 'They sewed up a cut, but Mummy will be her usual self in no time, you'll see.'

What is my "usual self" according to him, I wonder?

Oliver says ok and seems reassured, but Jack is quiet. I'm not even sure if he's still in the room – without hearing him it's impossible to know. We parted on bad terms, and I wonder whether he gave any thought to our argument while he was staying at Jamie's, or whether he forgot it straight away. He is hard to read these days, and I don't know if he will be upset by seeing me here, or whether he'll swallow it, as he seems to do everything else.

It's probably just his age, but Jack sometimes feels like a stranger. And when your little boy, who you carried and birthed and have loved and cared for every moment of his life shrugs you off like an old cardigan, it hurts. When he chooses friends and playing computer games over you, it's hard. I used to know him inside out, could predict what he would say and do in most situations, but these days his thoughts are hidden, his moods unpredictable. My life is a race against his hormones, which are always one step ahead. Sometimes it feels like

I will never truly know him again. Rather than being the centre of his world as I once was, I am now an irritation, an embarrassment, and he would rather spend time with Jamie.

Perhaps this gradual separation is a normal part of motherhood – children becoming independent so they can function in the world is the whole point after all. But it takes adjustment. It's like they're on a piece of elastic which stretches and stretches; the trick is to not let it snap. Jack is my learning curve, and every new stage or life experience he goes through is my first time as his guide. He made me a mother, he's the one with whom I have made the most mistakes, and as much as I feel guilty about all the trial and error with him, that is what created our bond.

Oliver is wittering on and on and it's a strain to tune in to Jack's voice, but, finally, I hear him talking with Jamie. They are being quiet so as not to wake me, which is lovely on one hand and annoying on the other, because their words are inaudible. However, Jack is obviously upset.

Cracking one eye a tiny bit, I see him standing with his arms around his father's waist. His face is buried in Jamie's chest. He is shuddering. Jamie has one arm slung across Jack's shoulders, and his free hand is rubbing Jack's hair. Jamie sways slightly, like he's holding a babe in arms.

This is unbearable. And it's all my fault.

Guilt demands that I open my eyes. But when I do, a few minutes later, none of them notice.

Jamie is flicking through one of my magazines, and Jack is in the armchair. Oliver is on his lap. That in itself is a miracle. Jack yawns, setting his brother off too, and it is clear how much the last few days have taken their toll; their drawn faces describe the worry I've put them through. Oliver's puffy eyes have dark circles underneath, and Jack scratches unconsciously at invisible rashes beneath his clothes.

They look sad and uncomfortable, out of place in this room, and I hate myself for putting them here. They are often at odds with each other but, at this moment, fear unites them.

I whisper hello, and Jamie looks round at me. The boys jump up and rush over. Oliver scrambles onto the bed while Jack leans across me in an awkward embrace. They can't know how much it hurts to be shifted about like this, but I don't let it show – they are happy to see me, and their reactions are so real, so honest, that joy spills down my cheeks.

It's hard to believe that just a week ago I was itching to get away from my children. How did I get to that point? They are innocent, vulnerable, and yes, they wind me up, but they also look to me for boundaries and examples. They are normal, complicated, emotional human beings, not demons, and never again will I feel burdened by the responsibility of motherhood. Love and guilt stun me in equal measures. All I can do is hug them close, and weep.

Hearing a little cough reminds me that Jamie is here too, standing at the foot of the bed. He must feel like an intruder. Suddenly I'm tired of playing games, of trying to second guess what he may or may not be thinking. Life can be snuffed out at a moment's notice, so what's the point of bullshit? I catch his eye and smile.

'How are you?' he asks.

'Ok. I've been better.' Speaking ravages my tender throat.

'They've been really worried about you,' he says. 'We all have. Your mum and dad wanted to come over with us, but I put them off. Just said I'd keep them informed. I hope that's ok?'

Ok? It's brilliant. Jamie knows that the last people I would want here are my parents, asking questions. Nodding, I whisper that it's fine.

Oliver is telling me about the flight over and how cool it was because he was allowed the window seat and could see everything, even houses and cars and people who looked like toys. Jack has recovered his composure now he can see I'm ok, and he chimes in too, over the top of Oliver, explaining again about the stunt nuts on his new bike and how Jamie took them to Castle Park, to go riding. I can't follow either of them properly; they are too fast, too keen, too fanatical, and their voices merge like birdsong.

Their constant vying for my attention has

started again straight away and I can't lie, it is disheartening, but although I'm exhausted and in pain, I absorb the moment. My throat is full of razor blades, so I can't say much, but they barely notice. Their incessant chatter makes me smile, which cracks my dry lips, but I can't help it. They're funny. When did I forget that?

All I need to do is raise my eyebrows and nod, making indistinct 'mmm' sounds when it seems appropriate; that's all the encouragement they need to describe every detail of the last six days. Jack is on one side of me, Oliver is on the other, and I'm holding their hands. It's like watching a tennis match, my throat pulling as I turn my head from side to side, but there are no words for this moment, no superlatives strong enough to describe it. I'm here in my hospital bed, bruised and sore, with my sons exuding love towards me. I could absorb it forever.

Wallowing in self-pity and destructive negativity has denied me the most precious and fulfilling relationship – that of a mother and her children. I've been the ultimate fool.

Death came close enough to touch, so I'm going to accept my second chance and make the most of my blessings. I'm young and healthy, with two bright, gorgeous, loving kids. I have a job and friends and a roof over my head. I have so much – why did I nearly throw it all away?

25

After Jamie and the boys left, I snoozed for a while. The clanging of dinner trolleys woke me, but nobody came in here so, when Meredith came back, I sent her to ask when I am allowed to eat.

She came back in with an apologetic face. 'They said you're on liquids only for the next 12 hours, I'm afraid.'

It makes sense, because my throat is incredibly sore, but a big, juicy burger with fries and mayonnaise would go down a treat right now. Still, she also said they told her the operation was successful; there should only be a tiny scar. My brain scan will be first thing tomorrow, then I can go when they are sure everything is fine.

Meredith tells me that she invited Jamie and the boys to stay at her house. That is kind of her, but I can't help wondering if it's because she still feels guilty. I don't blame her for what happened though, quite the opposite. I'm grateful to her in fact, for the journey I've been on. She taught me lessons I would not have learned otherwise. If I believed in it, I'd say that Fate brought me to France and made the two of us friends, but

I don't, because that would mean handing my decisions over to a higher power, when I must accept full responsibility for them.

However, Meredith has become important to me; we have been through a life-changing experience together, and I hope that we will stay friends. Her influence makes me braver and calmer, reminds me that there are other sides to life. She has been my confidante, my advisor and, ultimately, my saviour. I will never be one of The Perfects, but that's fine. The others are of no interest.

'So that's good, isn't it?' Meredith asks. 'Just a couple more tests and you'll be able to go home. I bet you can't wait to get back. I know I can't.'

'Yeah, I suppose.' My belly rumbles, and we laugh. 'But everything is different now.' It feels nice to speak, despite my gravelly throat.

'Surely you want to get out of here?'

'Of course. But there's a comfort in being looked after.'

She grins. 'You've become institutionalised. Even your stomach's responding.'

'Exactly. But it'll be weird going home because so much has happened. I can't imagine this fading into memory.'

Meredith rubs her eyes, smudging mascara into the bags beneath them. She is tired yet shows no signs of leaving. 'I know what you mean,' she says. 'It's like that for me too.'

She pauses, and her face brightens. 'You

know, Jamie and I were chatting earlier, and he still really cares about you.'

Shutting my eyes, I turn my head away. Now is not the time.

Meredith doesn't take the hint. 'I think it was great of him to bring the boys over and fend off your parents, don't you? He didn't have to do that.'

'Are you stirring?' I look back at her and shake my head. 'I hardly know my arse from my elbow at the moment, and you're matchmaking?'

She raises her eyebrows, smiles, and shrugs.

'He is my *ex*-husband.'

'But you've done nothing but talk about him from the minute we got here! I thought you were still in love with him.'

'Yeah, *you* thought. But I don't know what I think, or what I want.'

A cleaner comes in with a broom, and Meredith smiles at him. They chat while he gives my room a quick sweep, then she turns back to me.

'Look, I get that the whole Jamie thing is complicated and confusing. But it could be simple if you stop overthinking – it doesn't matter what anyone else says.'

There she goes again, reading my mind. 'I don't know.'

'And I thought we'd established that you regretted chucking him out like you did?'

'I do, but –'

'Tana,' she says quietly, 'this might be your chance to sort things out. You can start again.'

I don't know why Meredith is so keen for me to use this situation to my advantage, but it doesn't really matter because I can see her point. Jamie and I are both here, so, regardless of our feelings or what the outcome might be, we do have an opportunity to talk. The real question is whether I am ready.

By way of an answer, a huge yawn escapes my burning throat, and she smiles. Taking her keys from her bag, she straightens the magazines, smooths the blanket on my bed and tells me she'll be back tomorrow.

'Tonight though,' she says, 'I'll have another chat with Jamie. See what I can find out.'

After she leaves, although I am exhausted, I can't switch off. Today has been an absolute head spin. If this is the start of the rest of my life, I have stuff to work through – things buried deep which must come out if I am to move forward. It's daunting but I am determined to admit my truth, because that's the only way to make things right. My body is sore, my limbs are stiff, but I am alive and healing.

The only thing making me anxious, is what Jamie and Meredith will talk about. How much will she tell him, about my feelings, and about what I did to end up in hospital? Whilst fear suggests that she will spill everything, rationality says she won't. It's not Meredith's place to go meddling, and I don't think she's like that. Her intentions seem genuine.

The thing is, she thinks it will be simple for me and Jamie to patch things up, but she doesn't know what I know, and I don't even know what he knows – we may have been married, but our experiences of that marriage are different. If she is right and there is a possibility of us reconciling, things will not be as they were. I won't allow it. I am a different person. I know what I want, what I deserve.

Everything got so toxic between us at the end and, whilst I have consistently blamed Jamie for that, if my time in France has taught me anything, it's to own my mistakes. Fooling other people is duplicity; fooling yourself is stupidity.

When I force myself to examine how it all went so wrong, memory insists that my relationship with Jamie unravelled fast. But memory is blinkered and selective and, really, we fell apart in steps.

I failed to acknowledge the red flags because they weren't waving vigorously enough. I pretended that everything was alright. But it wasn't right for ages. I hadn't been right. Now I believe the end began when I was pregnant with Oliver.

The hormones second time around seemed different. With Jack I had gained weight of course, but with Olly it was almost sixty pounds, a huge amount, and I felt like a whale.

My self-esteem was destroyed. Uncomfortable, depressed, and paranoid, I felt judged if Jamie so much as looked at me, and I tensed up or moved away if he touched me. That was bad enough but after Oliver's birth things got worse. If pre-natal depression punched me, post-natal depression kicked.

Oliver was a gorgeous baby, happy and easy going, and Jack enjoyed having a brother to help look after. I loved us being a family of four. But Oliver was not much of a sleeper. During the day, when Jamie was at work, I had a baby to contend with as well as a five-year-old to take to school, pick up, feed, entertain, etc, and a house to run. During the night, I still had a baby to look after. Oliver's continual waking and difficulty settling again often meant that feeding and changing him took over an hour, and that could happen two or even three times a night. Sometimes he woke Jack, and I had to deal with him too. The worst of it was that Jamie slept through it all, like a hibernating bear. He awoke refreshed, while I barely knew day from night.

At first, I didn't question the routine. Hindsight says I should have expressed and bottled my milk so Jamie could share the burden. It is ridiculous, but I didn't do that because I thought he would hate me and Oliver, if he lost sleep. That's the truth. I had always felt unworthy of Jamie, so did everything to keep him, and that included sheltering him from the stress of a new-born. All the night-time jobs were mine. And all the day-time jobs were mine too. Even if I was unwell and struggling to get out of bed, Jamie would snore on, oblivious to the crying or calling which had awoken me.

As the weeks and months passed, overtiredness bordered delirium. My mental health deteriorated. Rational thought was impossible. Everyone in our house got the sleep they needed except me, and I was envious. Furious. Resentful. They all lived easy lives because I enabled it – but Jamie did not recognise this fact and I didn't point it out or ask for help. Admittedly, I would doze on a Saturday afternoon when he took them out, but he got all the fun, and I got all the drudgery.

Fatigue also played tricks with my emotions, which fluctuated like a springtime barometer. Despite pretending that I was fine, oftentimes I would be seething inside, running an internal dialogue of anger and misery completely at odds with my behaviour. When it got too much I would cry in the bathroom.

Not telling Jamie how I felt was foolish. It's as simple as that. He was not a mind reader, but I expected him to be. How could he understand my morning hostility, when he had slept, and I had been up several times? I should have said, I should have asked for help, but I didn't, and my biggest mistake was never rocking the boat. Ever scared of losing him, honestly believing that any complaint or suggestion of weakness would send him packing, I kept my grievances close and carried on.

Yes, I went to the park and toddler groups, and chatted with other mums, but because I was still very young, most were much older than me and I never felt we had much in common. Plus, none of them seemed to be struggling. At one baby group I went to, conversations centred on the joys and privileges of parenthood, and people's new, improved outlooks on life. I got sucked in, but milestone chats of crawling, walking, feeding, talking, was dull, dull, *dull*! All the mums there rejoiced in everything about motherhood, and their incessant conversations about bowel movements made me want to scream.

These days, there is so much honesty about the challenges of having young kids but, back then, nobody mentioned them. Now I realise that it was one-upmanship, a quest to be seen as perfect, no different to buying the most fashionable, expensive pram to parade your baby around town in. I suspect that inside they all felt like me and that we were, inadvertently, perpetuating a lie. Had we been brave enough to admit how hard it was and what a tough time we were having, we could have been open and shared ideas. I would not have felt alone.

Not only that, but I was damaging Jamie's relationship with the boys by not allowing him to do the harder jobs. It's taken me coming to France and letting him get on with it to see this. Suppressing my feelings also resulted in me taking exception to every little thing he did or said. He trod cautiously and asked if I was ok, and offered to help me out, but I would insist I was fine. As everyone knows, that is usually a lie. It means, 'I'm fuming.'

A wet towel left on the floor, toothpaste blobs in the sink, Jamie having a beer with his workmates at lunchtime … the list of things to rage about was long and varied. I resented that he had a life, while I felt isolated and swamped. Even his journey home from work, squashed in and smelling other commuters' armpits and bad breath, seemed like luxury time I could only dream of because all I knew was crying, feeding, and changing nappies.

I hated toys all over the floor and washing hanging from every radiator. I hated that a simple trip to the shops had to be planned to the last moment, to ensure neither child was hungry. Or tired. Or that Oliver didn't need changing. Imagining being able to jump into the car and go somewhere on a whim, without factoring in feeding and sleeping times and having a giant bag full of nappies, milk, toys, and clothes with me, was like imagining fairyland.

Now, please don't misunderstand me – I have always loved my children more than anything in the world, more than I could have believed possible – but by the age of twenty-three, I was washed up, wrung out and invisible. I had lost myself in loving them. Nobody remembered about me, the walking shadow. I barely remembered myself. In little chunks, I crumbled.

Drained and depleted, with a ruined body and low self-esteem, I relied on sugary snacks and coffee to keep me going. Of course, I knew I shouldn't. Of course, I knew I should use fresh air and exercise instead to help me feel good, but caffeine and cakes were a quick hit. They won every time.

I gained more weight, and the negative cycle continued, but my justification was that with life revolving around a baby and a small child, I was opting for the solution which made me temporarily happy.

The irony is that in trying to keep my husband, I pushed him away. Swallowing my feelings and projecting my insecurities onto him, I would accuse him of finding me unattractive. Pretty girls on the TV prompted snide comments about how he probably fancied them. The girls he worked with were a huge source of insecurity too, and I would question him: what are they like? Are they single? Are they attractive? Do they go to the pub at lunchtime too?

More than once, I asked him if he was having an affair. He would swear he wasn't, and swear he'd never do that because our little family made him so happy. But I wouldn't stop. In my mind, it was clear.

He was telling the truth, and I should have known it, because there was no evidence to support my accusations. I should have trusted him and examined my own wild imaginings instead, tried to see them for what they were. But I didn't. I couldn't. The mind is powerful. It makes you believe what you want to believe.

This went on for months, and the situation drip, drip, dripped until Jamie was tiptoeing around me, but my warped sense of reality told me his caution was guilt. Eventually, figuring that things could not get any worse, I decided we needed to have a proper argument, so called him at work.

I'd somehow fallen into the habit of phoning him repeatedly during the day, never considering how irritating or embarrassing it must have been, and I wanted to express my feelings right then and there. My logic was that if he was speaking to me, he was not kissing or flirting with someone else. Because, in my head, it was obvious that every woman he worked with was Jamie-hungry.

Anyway, on the day I decided to pop the abscess in our relationship, his new secretary answered. This was normal; her job was to field his calls and even I didn't have a direct number for him, but right then her voice grated. She was only about nineteen and I knew it was her first job because Jamie had told me but, instead of thanking her and leaving a message when she said he was unavailable, I demanded that she go and get him.

'I can't, I'm sorry,' she said. He's in an important meeting. They've been in there over an hour though, so hopefully it'll be over soon. I'll make sure he calls you.'

'Who else is in this meeting?' I asked.

'I'm sorry, I don't know all of their names,' she said. 'I've only been here a couple of weeks and haven't met everyone yet.'

'I didn't ask for your life story,' I said. 'I just want to know how much longer he'll be.'

'I'm really sorry but I'm not sure,' she said, her voice shaking. 'But I do know that the meeting is important.'

'Is it more important than me? His wife?'

'No, no, of course not. I didn't mean to imply that. It's just that it's all about projections and targets and portfolios, so it's best that I don't interrupt. I don't want to get into trouble. If you don't hear from him soon, maybe try again in an hour?'

Heat rose from my stomach, up my chest and throat to my face. How dare she not disturb the meeting? How dare Jamie not understand my misery? How dare I settle for this non-life?

Just as I envied Jamie his commute, I envied that young secretary. She had an office, a job, and free time. She probably wore a smart, tailored suit. She probably had manicured nails, expensive perfume, and a nice haircut. She probably strolled smugly around the city, shopping in her lunch hour.

In comparison, I had dull skin with hormonal spots, unwashed hair pulled back into a scraggy ponytail, and extra pounds of fat everywhere. Without showering that morning, I had donned grubby jogging bottoms, and an oversized T-shirt decorated with breast milk and baby vomit stains. No bra. My nails were bitten and ragged. To be able to wander around the city, even just window shopping, was pure fantasy.

The secretary's professionalism and politeness were sweet, but I knew she was trying hard to appease and then lose me – she just wasn't experienced enough to do it quickly. I could have been her, with qualifications, a decent job, and free weekends; instead, I had two kids, a mortgage, and all my family and friends were back in Cornwall.

I hated her for my life.

'Call back in an hour?' I sneered. 'Who the hell do you think you're talking to? I'm Jamie's *wife* and I want to speak to him. Don't tell me to call back.'

'Honestly, Mrs Malone, I am really sorry, but I can't interrupt their –'

'Listen here, girl. You get a message to him. I need him to call. I'm having a terrible day.'

'I'm awfully sorry Mrs Malone,' she

repeated, 'but I can't.'

'You can't? Or you won't?'

She swallowed. 'I'm not allowed to disturb their meeting. It's important.'

'Yeah, yeah, portfolios. Projections. You told me already. What are you hiding?'

'Hiding? What do you –'

'Why are you saying I can't speak to him? Are you covering up for him or something?'

'Please, Mrs Malone. I really don't understand. What do you mean?'

My hands curled into tight fists. 'I mean exactly what I asked. But, as you are being so difficult, I will make it even clearer.' Speaking slowly and loudly, I said, 'I think you are lying. Jamie is not in a meeting at all, but off somewhere with one of you sluts from the office.'

She did not respond.

'Nothing to say for yourself, eh?'

The silence grew.

'I'm right, aren't I?'

I heard quiet sniffing, but she still didn't speak.

'Are you shagging my husband? I know it's one of you.'

The dial tone was loud in my ear.

Remembering every hideous word now, I wonder why she didn't hang up earlier. At the time though, I just stared at the receiver, unable to believe that she had. Then, in a rage of screaming fury, I smashed the plastic receiver against the wall. Unable to destroy her, the phone had to do instead. It wouldn't break though, it wouldn't even crack, and that angered me even more. Eventually I stopped whacking it and burst into tears.

Around six o'clock, I was making dinner when Jamie slammed the front door, strode into the kitchen, and stared at me. 'What the hell is wrong with you?' he demanded. 'Seriously, what were you thinking?'

Turning away from him, I opened the oven to check my pie wasn't burning. The blast of heat felt like a just punishment.

'Tana, I'm talking to you. Why were you so rude to Jasmine?'

Oh, she would be called Jasmine, wouldn't she? Beautifully scented and pretty.

'I don't know,' I said, still not looking at him.

'When I came out of my meeting, she was crying so hard I thought someone had died. At first, she wouldn't tell me what had happened but, in the end, she admitted what you said. I was mortified. Why would you show me up like that?'

'I don't know. I didn't think.'

'I'm so confused. You called her a slut! Accused us both of having sex. What the fuck, Tana? You're unbelievable. Look at me, please!'

There was sadness and bewilderment in his eyes. His cheeks were flushed.

'She had no idea what you were going on about, and neither do I.' He tugged his tie off, and tossed it onto the kitchen table, shaking his head. The blonde streaks in his hair blazed under the lights. 'What's the matter?' he asked gently. 'This isn't you.'

It was as if all the air left my body. There was nothing I could say, because no words could justify my actions. Just as well the phone was still intact, otherwise I would have to explain that too.

It was the perfect opportunity for Jamie to admit any wrongdoings, or even say he wanted to break up, but he didn't. Instead, he wrapped his arms around me and held me as I fell to pieces. At that time, he was still faithful and honest, and I knew it. For a short time, the numerous affairs with multiple colleagues that I had been so certain about seemed ridiculous.

There was a moment when I considered sending Jasmine some flowers to say sorry, but despite knowing that she was not having an affair with my husband, I couldn't. I still hated her too much.

After that, even though we had talked, Jamie remained guarded. I had shown him a side of me he hadn't known was there – and in retrospect I can understand his reaction. He became overly polite, avoiding all conflict, and I didn't know how to make things relaxed again.

It didn't take long for me to convince myself that he hated me for what I had done to Jasmine; I was sure he no longer trusted my behaviour, and my paranoia steadily increased. I shut down, became less balanced, began imagining affairs again, and stretched the distance between us in the process.

I created our reality. Maybe not completely, because both of us should have tried to heal our fractured relationship, but I admit I was selfish, demanding, jealous and irrational. Inadvertently, I pushed Jamie to seek affection elsewhere. That is the truth. Why wouldn't he do what he was suffering for anyway?

Splitting up wasn't what I wanted, it wasn't what I intended, but it happened. Through a lack of communication though, not a lack of love. We never had the conversations that mattered, the difficult ones that would have hurt. And that was my fault.

Why has it taken a near-death experience to make me understand what I did? And who came to me the first moment he could?

On the night we broke up, when he came home late, looking dishevelled, I made him leave and I slammed the door. I refused to talk to him. His admission about Rose hurt me so deeply that forgiveness was not an option, and I wouldn't dream of giving him a second chance. Instead, I avoided him and ignored his calls. For several months I wouldn't even let him see Jack and Oliver.

That's how awful I was. It wasn't their fault, they wanted to see him and were confused about where he had gone and why, yet I made them suffer too. As shameful as it is to admit, I must. I must own the fact that I was one of those spurned women who, out of spite and bitterness, punish their partners using their children.

Really, we were all punished.

I hated him for sure. But I never, ever stopped loving him.

26

A noisy MRI machine is scanning me. It's claustrophobic in here. Forced to be still, I want to wriggle and stretch out, as long as a spill, and itches have sprung up in every place imaginable.

It's not all physical either – my mind is jumping through hoops, wondering what Jamie and Meredith talked about last night. Because they don't know each other, I doubt she grilled him for information about his feelings and, knowing Jamie, I doubt he would have admitted much even if she had. But Meredith does have a way of reading people and bringing them out of themselves, so it's possible she managed to glean something interesting.

Either way, I can't wait to hear what she has to tell me, and it's nice that probably for the first time, I am not torturing myself by assuming he fancies her, or that they slept together. He is here because he cares about me. It's as simple as that.

I'm confident that the MRI will be fine, and I doubt the drugs did anything permanent. I wouldn't be healing so quickly if they had. I do know how lucky I am though. Only two days ago I was in intensive care, in an induced coma, so under the circumstances, I'm doing alright. Better than that, I'm doing well, and I am grateful.

Everyone has options to change; every new day brings the possibility of a fresh start, but we get so caught up in the day-to-day that we lose sight of that fact. We often only realise it when something major happens – and I am no exception. But while this opportunity is fresh in my mind, I am seizing it. Tomorrow is today, beginning with how I speak to myself; negative and derogatory will become kind and understanding. Hopefully.

Alongside keeping my inner monologue in check, I will get healthy. I will savour my life and energy and body; I'll appreciate everything they offer. I will investigate that Law degree. I will restart my career path. I will get out with Nicky and the girls from work regularly. Jamie will see the boys more. The nightly wine drinking will stop, and I will eat fresh food. I will treat myself to regular haircuts and new clothes. I might even look up Sarah on Facebook – offer an olive branch.

These changes will add up to a huge difference.

Right now, my muscles and joints are sore, in fact every part of me aches and feels weak, but I will push past the pain and keep moving. I will get strong through exercise; I'll stretch. I'll take time to smell the rain. Moving hurts, but I couldn't do it when I first woke up. And if I hadn't woken up, I wouldn't be doing it at all.

After the MRI nobody looks concerned, so I assume everything is fine. I'm sure Meredith or the doctors will confirm later. Back in my room, the nurse does all her usual checks, then removes my drip and catheter. I am free. She raises the back of the bed, fluffs up my pillows, and hands me a glass of orange juice. Like a miracle, I can grasp it and lift it to my lips. The most delectable thing I've ever tasted.

The nurse also gets my phone from my bag. There are several messages from my parents, but I will look at those when I'm ready – it's the one from Meredith saying she is taking Jack and Oliver out for ice cream so Jamie and I can talk which grabs my attention. She doesn't say when.

Immediately I'm back in panic mode. I am not prepared … I look awful … I can't do this … I am not ready. Her words blur on the screen and my head whirls with reasons why Jamie and I should not have this time, why it will go wrong.

But what was I just saying? What promises did I just make? This 'doom' way of thinking must stop. Breathing deeply and slowly, I repeat in my head that things are different. I am different.

To be honest, I must stop fearing myself. Stop limiting myself. Had I done that in the first place, maybe none of this would have happened. What is fear, after what I have been through?

Nothing is scarier than almost dying.

Get off the side-lines, Tana. Stop sulking. Stop blaming everyone else for the fact that you haven't joined in the game.

I am apprehensive though, and that's allowed, because when Jamie and I talk, our conversation is bound to be awkward. Who knows what turns it might take? Jagged wounds are bound to be reopened. But maybe then, they'll heal properly. We will discuss everything in due course, and I promise I will be honest. But we can't do it all at once. The conversation will unfold as it must.

However, he is coming to see me, and making myself presentable is another issue entirely. With a fresh operation site on my throat, bruising and cuts on my face, and greasy hair clumped with dried blood, I am not looking my best. Confidence can only come from damage limitation, which means getting out of bed and into the bathroom.

Pressing the button makes the bed head lift further and my cracked ribs scream. Pain stabs in every direction. Dizziness and nausea wash over me and black spots dance in my eyes. Gasping, clutching my side, I breathe slowly until it all subsides.

When I shift sideways on the bed the room tilts, and fresh waves of sickness crash through me. This is a very slow process. But once acclimatised to the new position, I lower my feet and feel the cool hardness of the floor. Edging my backside forward bit by bit, at last, I stand.

Then gravity pulls at my injuries, forcing me to sit back down. Tears sting – all I want to do is get my bag from the cabinet and cross to the bathroom. It is a matter of metres but feels like a mile with an obstacle course thrown in for good measure. Every muscle in my body has seized, the operation site is angry, and there is sandpaper in my throat. My journey across the room may as well be across the Andes.

I must do this though – and I will. That mirror needs to show me the truth. Childbirth hurt much more. Come on, get a grip. Movement heals.

Breathing as deeply as my ribs will allow, I stand and let the dizziness subside before taking six tiny, shuffling steps to the cabinet. Sweating and panting, I get my bag.

There is no makeup in it, but there is my hairbrush, some lip balm, and a tube of tinted moisturiser. They will have to do. A hairband at the bottom is a good find; Jamie always liked my hair in a ponytail.

Wincing with every step, I hobble to the bathroom and use the toilet, wash my hands, and smooth some moisturiser across my face, avoiding the stitches and bruising. A slick of lip balm makes me more presentable. In old films, the ladies pinch their cheeks to add colour, so I try that, and it works a bit – I'm less white and purple, although the swelling still looks bad. It's true to say I've looked better, but this will have to do. It's better than making no effort at all.

Preparing to see Jamie today feels almost as traumatic as when we first got together. Back then, I would spend hours bathing, shaving my legs, trimming and polishing my nails, exfoliating my face, and using a mud mask with cucumber slices and moisturisers. My parents would yell at me, and I'd be at fever pitch by the time he rang the doorbell.

In those days we were romantic, our time was precious. Then real life and responsibility broke us apart. I wonder whether we'll be able to get past the bad feeling to find the old magic. And, if we can, should we try again or let it lie?

Lifting my arm to brush my hair hurts my ribs, so I'm just trying to coax it to look in any way presentable. Suddenly he is there, behind me in the mirror. With a squawk which turns into a gasp of pain, I spin around to face him. A flash of burning sears my chest and throat, and my hairbrush skitters across the floor.

'Sorry,' he says, moving towards me with arms outstretched, frowning with concern. But he stops just as quickly and drops his arms. 'I didn't mean to make you jump.'

Jamie is wearing dark blue jeans and a red sweatshirt which makes his blonde hair even more striking. As I absorb how handsome he is, a rush of heat flushes through my body. My cheeks burn.

It could be the anaesthetic or the pain or the embarrassment of standing here looking so horrific in nothing but a hospital gown with a slit up the back, but my head starts spinning and I grab the doorframe for support. I am not ready for him to be this close. He had his arms open though, and I know that if he were to hold me, I would melt in his arms and never want to solidify.

It is a punch, how everything that was once natural between us is now uncomfortable and wrong. How so much of that is my fault.

'Tana, are you ok?' Jamie steps back, giving me space. 'I'm sorry, I shouldn't have come.'

The last thing I want is for him to leave. 'No, you're fine.' Mustering a smile, I say, 'It's ok – I'm just still getting used to standing. It makes me a bit woozy.' Taking shallow breaths, I clasp the wood and concentrate on how smooth the gloss paint feels beneath my fingertips.

'Well, let me get that for you.' He picks up my hairbrush and hands it to me with a grin. 'Here. I wouldn't want to cause you any embarrassment.'

My cheeks burn hotter as I squash my smile, but I know he is talking about my gown – if I bent down, it would open at the back. We were always on the same wavelength, and the absurdity of my outfit can't be ignored.

Our fingers touch as I take the brush from

him and our eyes lock for a moment too long. His mouth is so familiar, so inviting and, oh God, I want to kiss him so much. My whole body is tingling. But I look at the floor, murmur my thanks, and angle myself so he can't see anything. Then begins the long journey back across my room.

Shuffling backwards, like a butler from the Queen, I notice his small smile and wonder if he feels the electricity too, because he is rocking on his feet and when I reach the bed, he holds out a hand.

'Here, let me –' he starts, then stops. He drops the hand and watches instead, biting his lip and wincing with me as I ease myself onto the bed.

My cracked ribs yell as I settle my weight, and although I am trying not to cry, I can't help the strange squeaking sound that comes out of my mouth. Jamie starts forward, as if to help, but stops again.

'I'm fine,' I gasp. 'Take a seat. And help yourself to a drink if you want one.' I nod towards the cabinet, with its plastic jug of lukewarm tap water.

Shaking his head, he says, 'Thanks, but I just had a coffee with Meredith.'

Straight away, I wonder what he thinks of her, whether he finds her attractive. I know this is precisely the kind of thinking I must stop, but it's hard. Insecurity is my default. Taking controlled breaths, pushing the air out through pursed lips, I manage the pain and breathe, until both body and mind feel ok. Jamie waits.

Once I'm more comfortable, we catch up on how the boys have been behaving; Jamie says that they had been having a fantastic time before Meredith called him, and I assume he means I ruined it.

'You didn't have to come.'

He frowns and his eyes narrow. 'There's no way we wouldn't have. We were worried about you. I just meant it's been great.' There is a shadow in his eyes. 'I've loved having them.'

My stomach flips. 'I'm glad,' I say, and look away, realising how true it is. 'You need to see them more.' I meet his eyes and nod. 'You really do.'

'That'd be amazing.' He smiles properly, a face-lightening smile, and his eyes sparkle.

We sit in silence for a while. The window is open, and sunlight is streaming through, warming my back. Jamie's hair looks like spun gold. The tree is full of twittering, chattering birds and I wish our conversation could flow as easily, but I don't know what to say. Perhaps the drugs and medication have affected my brain after all because the only words pressing to be spoken are completely inappropriate.

I love you.

Please hold me.

Kiss me.

I ask him what he told the boys, about why I'm in hospital and he shrugs. 'To be honest, I don't know a lot.' Shaking his head, he says, 'When Meredith rang, I was too shocked to ask questions and she still hasn't told me any details.'

He leans back in the armchair, rests one foot on his other knee and drums his fingers on the wooden arm rest. 'I told them what she told me, that you'd had an accident and hurt your head. They were upset though – Jack especially.'

'Really? Jack was upset?' My tears well unexpectedly.

Jamie nods, then hangs his head and wrings his hands together. 'Yeah, he was. He asked if you were going to die.'

Now the tears spill. It is horrible, knowing that my brash, independent son feared for my life. It sounds absurd to admit, but I have never really considered how much the boys love and need me, especially Jack, because we spend so much time squabbling. Our relationship feels based on attrition, not love.

Jamie is not trying to make me feel guilty – he is simply answering my question – but I deserve to feel this way. I have made terrible mistakes, and these tears are for everything that has happened over the past few years. He edges the armchair closer, leans forward, and props his elbows on his knees. His fingers make steeples.

But I cannot look him in the eye.

Covering my face with my hands, I sob out

all the humiliation and regret until my ribs are on fire, and it feels like someone is sanding the inside of my throat. I forget about how I look, what I think and feel, and almost forget he's there, until I hear the chair scrape backwards and feel him sit gently on the bed beside me. His arms wrap me. Jamie has pushed aside our bad history and is treating me just as he would any other person in pain – with strong, silent support. Slumped into him, I let the burning pain in my ribs and throat incinerate the past.

Time rushes backwards to when I was sixteen, sitting on my bed in Newquay, with a third positive pregnancy test in my hand. My world was upside down then, and this situation feels similar. At that time, despite the conflicting thoughts and worries, the decision-making, and the fear that my parents would kill or disown me, one constant remained: Jamie.

His arms encircled me then as they do now, his hands stroked my hair then as they are doing now, and his calming voice said everything would be alright, just like now. Jamie understands my pain because he shares it – we are both Jack's parents and neither of us want to see him hurting.

It feels so right being in Jamie's arms once more, so familiar and safe, yet different. Like a favourite song with a new arrangement.

When I'm all cried out, neither of us move. My head is nestled into his shoulder and his sweatshirt is wet, but we don't break the moment. Too much time has been wasted already; here and now is all that matters. I will *not* let the past haunt my future. Whatever will be shall be.

'I'm sorry, Jamie,' I whisper. 'I got hurt taking cocaine. Meredith didn't tell you.'

He twists towards me, gently tilting my chin up so he can look at me. 'You're kidding? You took coke? Why?'

I have no answer. When I can bear to meet his eyes, they are dark and questioning. 'What's this all about, Tana?' he asks quietly. 'You hate drugs.'

'I don't know.' My words have dried on my lips. Whatever I say will sound pathetic, inadequate to the job of justification, but I owe him something so take a deep breath and carefully sit up straighter.

'It's hard to explain. I needed space. The boys are hard to cope with. I've been down. Really down.'

Admitting this is difficult, but if I don't speak the truth there is no point in saying anything.

'Well, why didn't you ask me? I'd have them anytime. But I mean – cocaine? You've always been so anti. Why would you do that?' He moves back to the armchair, leaving me alone on the bed. 'Come on, talk to me.'

Rubbing my eyes, I wonder how I can make

any of it make sense. Away from the heat of the moment, and knowing the consequences, I can't rationalise anything – not my mindset, my jealousy, or my fear of missing out. I could say I got swept along with the tide, but that would be a lie because I jumped right in.

Without an answer I just shrug, wincing again at the pain that shoots through my ribcage. One day I'll tell him everything, I know I will. It is important to, because in a roundabout way he helped put me here. Many small pieces add up to make a heavy load, and I was overburdened. Right now, though, I can't think straight.

To be fair, Jamie doesn't press me on it. 'You said about me having the boys more,' he says. 'Can we work a new schedule – one that gives you more time for you, and me more time with them?'

'Yes.' I nod, looking at my hands in my lap.

'That's fantastic, thanks. You know, if you had asked me to help you, I would have.' His voice drops and he sighs. When I raise my eyes, he is looking at me intently. 'I've always wanted to see them more.'

This is something I've wondered about from the moment I threw him out. I thought he didn't want equal access because he didn't ask for it. 'Then why didn't you say anything?' I whisper. 'Why didn't you contest the divorce?'

Jamie sighs again and scratches the back of his neck. 'I don't know. I was stupid not to.'

'Because you didn't ask, I assumed you didn't want the responsibility – I figured you wanted a new life. I kept them to protect them.'

Jamie snaps his head up and stares at me, mouth wide open, brows furrowed. His teeth are exposed. Hugging himself, he shakes his head slowly, as if to let my words drop in. 'You thought I didn't love them? That I wouldn't take care of them?'

Shame lights my cheeks. My mouth is dry. What I just said was true, but only in part. Ignoring the sharpness in my throat, I swallow hard and turn away, to look through the window. I wish I were outside. The atmosphere in here is stale.

Realising I may have just ruined any chance of reconciliation, I consider how to reply – but I must be wholly truthful. I will not keep denying my feelings to placate others. Jamie and I have been estranged for a long time so there is nothing to lose. Straightening my back, I look him in the eye. 'Yes. Kind of.'

His eyes flash dark so I speak quickly to stop him protesting. 'I know I was wrong, but it's what I feared at the time.' It feels incredible to be saying this to him at last. 'You rejected me, Jamie. You hurt me more than you could ever know, and I wanted to hurt you back for abandoning us.'

'Abandoning?' His face is contorted. 'What do you mean?'

'Rejection *and* abandonment.' It takes very

little effort to remember the way I felt, and now the cork has been popped, my words are bubbling over. 'Don't pretend, Jamie. You chose to spend your time with someone else. Not your mates playing football or some elderly neighbour who needed a few chores doing, but a younger, prettier woman, who flattered and adored you. She had no children and no responsibilities. With her, you forgot about your own. That's what I mean.'

He crumples and exhales sharply, pressing his lips into a thin, bloodless line. Tears glimmer in his eyes as he stares at the crooked picture on the wall. The temptation to keep talking, to layer more accusations, more blame, more guilt on top of what I've already said is huge. But this is the new me; say what you mean, don't repeat it ten times.

'I didn't contest anything in the divorce,' he says at last, through tight lips, 'because I didn't want it to become uglier than it already was. I didn't want you to hate me any more than you already did.' There is such sadness in his voice that I want to pull him close, stroke his hair. But I don't.

'I figured that sooner or later we'd be able to work something out,' he says. 'We were always good at solving problems.' When he looks at me, his eyes are wet. He shakes his head. 'But that never happened.'

Rubbing his face as if trying to wash away

a stain, he says, 'I figured in the end that too much damage had been done – that it was best to agree with everything you wanted to avoid more drama. That's why I've just made sure to call them every day, even if I couldn't see them.'

This feels like the right time to ask. I must know. Trying to keep my voice calm and neutral, I finally ask the question that has been burning me for years. 'Why did you do it, Jamie? Why did you have an affair?'

Although I have realised a lot of this for myself, I need to hear it from him. I also want to know if Meredith's 'because he could' theory is right.

'I don't know. It seems so long ago, so senseless. I was a fool.' He runs his fingers through his beautiful hair again. 'You were unhappy and nothing I did seemed good enough. I thought you blamed me for Jack, and hated how your life had turned out. I didn't know what to do. I was lonely and felt rejected too.'

'You could have talked to me. Tried to help.'

'I know. I should have but didn't know how. I hoped it would pass – and then there was that call to my work. It just got worse and worse … I was furious but didn't know what to do about any of it.'

'How would being with someone else make it better?' I should stop these digs, but they've been barbs in my side for so long that they need to come out. We need this.

He holds his elbows and squeezes tight, then shrugs. 'It wouldn't. It didn't. Of course not. It's hard to explain but I'll be honest, I enjoyed getting attention from someone. You were a closed book to me, Tana. I didn't mean for anything to happen, it just did. Then, before I knew it, the whole situation got out of hand. Rose wanted to call and tell you. There was no way I would let that happen ... but I was too scared to do it myself.'

He looks me in the eyes and holds my hands in his, gently rubbing his thumb over my fingers. 'I wanted to confess everything, and see if we could straighten things out, but lacked courage. She and I had a massive row about it, and she finished the relationship the night you made me leave. I told you that – it's why I was home late.'

Strangely, I am not angry anymore. I don't feel sorry for him either. Just deflated.

'One more question. Was it just her, or were there more? I need to know.'

Shaking his head, he says, 'No, it was just her. And it was all wrong from the word go.' He holds my gaze with sorrowful eyes. 'I'm sorry, Tana. I'm really, really sorry. I never meant to hurt you all.'

There is nothing more to say. We sit in silence, while I mull over what's been said and wonder where we go from here. Hearing that Rose was the only one helps, even though I think his reason for prolonging the affair is nonsense.

But to be honest, there is no reason I would accept, and I also know the truth about my own behaviour. It must have been depressing living with me. I understand why he thought I didn't love him anymore. If only I had told him. If only I had explained. We both made communication mistakes that have brought us here.

'I've always loved you, Tana,' he says quietly, stroking my hair away from my face. He is looking at me with such sincerity that my eyes fill with tears again. 'It was always you,' he says, smiling. 'Ever since you got naked on the beach to get my attention.'

It's hard to believe this is happening but I can't help grinning too, picturing the scene. 'I was trying to save your life!'

We hold each other's gaze, both lost in the memory. Then he stands and tilts my chin up.

'You did save my life – I just didn't know it. Cheating was the biggest mistake I ever made. It was hard, having the kids so young, wasn't it? Especially for you. I didn't realise how alone you were.'

'Yeah,' I say. 'Good old retrospect.'

He wipes my cheek with his thumb. 'I know what you sacrificed. But we had something special, don't you think?'

I am glad that Jamie recognises how much my life changed in comparison with his. And I do think we had something special – I always thought so. But whether we can rekindle it is another matter.

'I'd like to try again,' he says. 'This happening to you has made me realise what I lost, and I don't want to lose you again. What do you say?'

My chest tightens and white brain fog obliterates coherent thought. He has just said the words I've wished to hear for years, so why can't I respond? On one level, I am aware that my mouth is opening and closing, froglike. On another, I don't care because I'm trying to decide.

My fear is that the ghosts of our past will haunt us forever. Not only that, but Meredith has inspired me, and I know now that I am capable of more than I believed. During this week away, I started looking forward and making decisions about the future; I don't want anything to complicate those plans. If Jamie comes back into my life, will I see them through or will I get distracted, and put my wants and needs aside like I always used to?

Slipping back into our old rhythms is probable but it would get me nowhere. I still love Jamie, that's not changed. I still want Jamie – going with Stefan underscored that. But realisation rugby tackles me: I don't *need* Jamie.

The air feels thick. Silence is hanging. He is gauging my reaction, lip clamped between his teeth, head tilted. And, as my face has probably displayed each thought like a billboard, it is little wonder he is studying me. But what did he expect? If he thought he could just sweep along here, say his magic words and snap me back under his spell, he was wrong.

To be fair, I was too. I didn't know how strong I am, how much I have changed.

Pacing across my hospital room, Jamie rubs his head, pulling his hair gently, then comes to stand in front of me. His neck and cheeks look flushed.

'I'm sorry if I spoke out of turn,' he says. 'But I needed to tell you what I feel. There's no pressure. We can take things as slowly as you like, day by day, if you want to. I just want the four of us to be together again. I miss us.'

I do too, but wonder if he really understands what he's asking. Which 'us' does he mean? Looking at his handsome face, the face that has filled my mind ever since we met, I want to shout 'Yes!' and throw myself at him. But I can't let emotion dictate my future this time. If this is going to happen, it must be right. I am not a kid anymore.

'What do you say, Tana?'

Taking a deep breath, I nod. 'I'd like that,' I say. 'But I have made plans for my future. I am going to start studying. My life needs to change – I'm getting qualifications and a career.'

He raises his eyebrows. 'Law?'

'Yep. Now the boys are older, I can fit in my studies around them. There are loads of options available you know, like night classes or distance learning.'

He looks genuinely pleased. 'It's a brilliant idea. When did you decide this?'

'A few days ago, before all this nonsense.' I flap my hand at the hospital bed. 'Meredith made me realise that I can.'

Jamie's smile could set a room on fire. 'That's great. She seems like a cool woman.'

'She is,' I say, nodding. 'She's awesome.'

Pouring himself a cup of water, Jamie takes a sip and licks his lips. 'I have seen her at school before but didn't realise you were such good friends.'

'We're not – well, we weren't.' The thought of Meredith being my friend makes me smile. 'I'm only here with her because of a random string of events. Coincidences, if you like.' Jamie frowns. 'I'll explain everything to you, the whole lot, don't worry. But she's part of my life now, for sure.'

I yawn, and wince because it hurts my throat.

'I'd better go,' Jamie says, 'let you get some rest. Your plan is brilliant though, Tana. You should do it.' He pats his pockets, checks his watch.

'I will. I'm going to makc lot of changes.'

He nods. 'You never know, it's so early in the school year that you might be able to join a class in the next couple of weeks. I'll help any way I can.'

'Thanks, I appreciate it – but one step at a time, yeah? My pace?'

'Absolutely.' Smiling, he holds his hands up, palms towards me. 'Everything at your pace.' It's like he's smiling at me for the first time. 'After you've recovered, we'll go out for that family pizza.'

'I'd like that,' I say again. 'The boys would too. They miss you. In fact, before I came away, Jack was asking if he can live with you.'

Taking my hands, Jamie helps me to my feet. 'Yeah, he told me. I was non-committal; said we'd talk about it with you. Maybe we can work out a half and half-type thing?'

I nod and he kisses my cheek. The familiar touch of his lips reminds me of our first kiss, by his car, outside my house. Textbook.

'Get some sleep,' he says. 'I'll come back tonight with the boys, if that's ok? Meredith said she wants to come too – she needs to speak to someone about getting you out of here. Then we can take it one day at a time. Slow as you like.'

'I can't wait,' I say. 'Thanks, Jamie. I appreciate you coming.'

He smooths my hair away from my face, tucks a strand behind my ear and smiles again. His eyes are shining, honest. 'Me too. Now, get some sleep.'

In the doorway, he turns and raises his hand. I mirror him, then sit back on my bed and listen until his footsteps fade.

THE END

About The Author

Kate Brazier is a London-based English teacher with a lifelong passion for Literature, and a Master's degree in Creative Writing. She is married and has three adult children.

If you enjoyed Tana's story, please leave a review on Amazon and/or Goodreads, because *A Week at Meredith's* is Kate's first novel, and she would be very grateful! You can her follow her on Amazon and on Facebook – search Kate Brazier Writer.

Printed in Great Britain
by Amazon